TOM LIGGETT

MOZART
IN THE
GARDEN

SILICON

VALLEY

AND ME,

WE GREW UP

TOGETHER

PRINTER'S DEVIL
P R E S S

Mozart in the Garden
© 2020 Tom Liggett

I have attempted to re-create the scenes and people from my childhood. The memories are real and vivid. They are, however, entirely mine. If anyone takes offense, that's too damn bad.

All images are from the author's personal collection.

ISBN (print, soft cover): 978-1-7334358-0-2
ISBN (ebook): 978-1-7334358-1-9
ISBN (audiobook): 978-1-7334358-2-6

Cover and interior design by www.DominiDragoone.com
Editorial services by Sandra Wendel, Write On, Inc.
Cover photos: Boy © hjalmeida/iStock; Tree © Anna Usova/iStock
Author photo by Eric Seymour

Published by
Printer's Devil Press
www.PrintersDevilPress.com
TomLiggett@sbcglobal.net

To Patricia Martinez,
because you enjoy my writing more than anyone I know.

CONTENTS

1 Cowboys, Indians, and Poor White Trash 1

2 Moves: Sexual and Otherwise 23

3 American Dreams Built on Pillars of Smoke 43

4 Green Grass Prison Walls 59

5 A Witch's Cottage in Hell's Most Distant Suburb 73

6 Weaker Than Most Boys/Stronger Than Most Men 83

7 Paradise Lost in a Green Velvet Box 93

8 All of My Names End with Mariah 103

9 The Human Punching Bag 117

10 Working More/Still Poor 137

11 Martian Living in a Tin Can 147

12 "No place that had hurricanes or goddamned snow" 169

13 Gold Dust Dreams and Hooker's Schemes 179

14 Of Tile Molds and Strawberry Pots 191

15 The Gatekeeper's Cottage 211

16 Once a Mountain, Now a Mole Hill 225

17 *Cleopatra* and Max 235

18 The End of the Grand Times 251

19 Life after Faye 265

    About the Author 279

1

COWBOYS, INDIANS, AND POOR WHITE TRASH

Silicon Valley. What a great name. It requires just two words to describe the world's favorite economic hotspot. Most people believe this wealth is a new thing. Every schoolchild knows the story: Steve Jobs entered central California, wiped out the indigenous residents, and transformed the place into Silicon Valley. Kind of like what happened when Moses led the Israelites into the Promised Land, but with fewer people of Hebrew extraction. More blonds. More software engineers too.

Truth be told, the Santa Clara Valley has been ground zero for many exceptional activities. The most productive mines in California were there. The valley's electronics industry led the world out of several economic recessions. But the Santa Clara Valley was once tops in another field too: agriculture. The soil and climate in that place are second to none. Grain, nuts, rose plants, grapevines, and fruit trees grew like nowhere else on earth. In the 1890s, more plant nurseries were situated in the greater San Jose area than anywhere in America.

Most of the Santa Clara Valley's agricultural production was beneficial to mankind. Some was not. German chemists purchased all the apricot, peach, and prune pits they could get from Santa Clara Valley fruit processors. The processors thought the Germans were crazy to buy worthless fruit pits. German chemists thought otherwise; they turned prune and apricot seeds into Zyklon B. Cyanide gas. The Nazis used that stuff to kill millions of people who were noted as being problematic. Twisted people can always find ways to corrupt beautiful things.

After World War II, the Santa Clara Valley grew new crops: houses, roads, industrial parks, and shopping centers. They were built to accommodate a pent-up demand for the good life. America was filled with people who had lived through the Great Depression and World War II. They wanted to party and raise kids, West Coast–style. That required brand-new, ranch-style, four-bedroom homes and high-paying jobs. Most of those new home buyers were not California natives. Many were former soldiers and sailors who had passed through the region during the war. They dutifully returned home after they were discharged from the military, but quickly learned that things were not the same.

Many people discovered that no other place could outshine California. People from all over the world poured into that fabled state. That influx led to a strange eventuality: most of the people who have lived in California weren't born there. They are transplants. Excepting me and a few other natives.

I had a strange entrance into the warm California sunlight. My mama was in the habit of marrying cowboys. While that created fast times for her, it caused a lot of trouble for me. Myron Thomas Liggett was the cowboy who rode through my mother's life just long enough to create me under an apricot tree. That's a lot of name to say in one mouthful. I ought to know, because I am Myron Thomas Liggett Junior. My father and I chose simpler names for day-to-day usage. My father called himself MT. I am plain ol' Tom.

MT Liggett was a perfect model for the stereotypical American cowboy. He seemed to personify the best and worst attributes of that type. MT was raised on the high southwest Kansas plains. That region is best defined by what is sometimes called the buffalo grass controversy. The proponents of that concept believe the combination of hideous weather, poor soil, and the lack of reliable quantities of water render the area unsuitable for permanent human habitation. Some people say that Kiowa County, Kansas, should have been left in its natural, undeveloped state. Area residents believe otherwise. They say the place is just fine.

Popular American lore indicates that every cowboy needs an Indian to conquer or a white woman to rescue. My mother was both. Her name was Lita Faye Snow. She was sixteen when she met MT Liggett in the summer of 1949. A Disney-produced, late-1940s American dream version of MT's sudden arrival would require that he meet her at the corner drugstore or a dance. In that type of fiction, he would have asked her to go out for a glass of Coca-Cola and a walk around the block. The details of their initial interaction were grittier.

MT got kicked out of the family home in Kansas immediately after he graduated from high school. He joined the navy. MT, at eighteen, was just out of basic training when he was transferred to Moffett Field Naval Air Station in Sunnyvale, California. He was away from home for the first time. MT had overactive hormones. In that regard, he was surrounded by fellows of like mind. MT asked the other sailors where he might find a ready piece of ass.

An older sailor named Tommy Tomlinson approached MT and said, "I've got a sister-in-law named Gladys Pierce. She's a grass widow." Just for the record, that type of widow is created by a divorce decree, not by death. Tommy Tomlinson told MT, "Gladys will spread her legs for you. But you will have to give her some money to speed the courtship."

That detail was not a hindrance to MT. He quickly traveled across the Santa Clara Valley to Gladys's house.

I can imagine what MT must have been thinking as he walked up to the bordello door: I'm not gonna be gettin' me a spring chicken here. She's had about six kids. Her pussy's so big, I'll probably have to tie a two-by-four to my ass to keep from falling in. But I'm so damned horny, my nuts are about to explode. Right now, I'd fuck a snake, if you held it down for me.

But things didn't work out that way. The brothel door was opened by Lita Snow, the prostitute's niece. MT immediately forgot about the prostitute. He had good reason for that lapse. Lita shocked MT's senses. She was the object of every heterosexual man's wildest fantasy. Lita and two of her sisters were beautiful. But they went beyond all normal definitions of beauty. They had angel faces and goddess bodies.

Lita was the prettiest girl in that bunch. She was just sixteen, but her looks were backed with experience—lots of experience. She had been with plenty of men and boys. You might expect that from a girl who was raised in a de facto brothel that contained three beautiful understudies.

I'm not saying Lita was a prostitute during that period. Who knows? She probably was, on one level or another. Truth be told, Lita's amorous enthusiasm derived from another quarter—she liked men. She liked the way they looked, talked, smelled, and

Royal "Tommy" Tomlinson. My maternal grandmother's third husband. My mother's stepfather. Tommy Tomlinson was a card cheat, small-time con man, small-time pimp, child molester, tightwad, pervert, bully, all-purpose son of a bitch, and main savior of my mother's family. Circa 1948. Campbell, California.

◇◇◇

Lita (left) and her sister Betty Snow Kirkley. The combination of fawning men and man-hating women created a toxic stew that poisoned succeeding generations of my mother's family. This evil was perpetuated by gorgeous young women who got away with far more than should have been allowed. From puberty onward, people cut those gorgeous women a lot of slack. Circa 1953.

◇◇◇

Lita and her sister Monnie. This flawed photograph does not reveal the true gorgeousness of the youngest Snow family beauty. Note the American Indian/Asiatic cast to her eyes. Monnie was lovely to look at and a lot of fun at a party, but she had her own special way of hating men and children.

Earliest existing photograph of my mother, Lita Snow. Lita was only about four years old when this photograph was taken, but she had already suffered through bouts of malaria and rickets. The latter disease was caused by the sparse, vitamin-deficient diet Lita and her siblings were fed.

◇◇◇

I have been around many families in cowboy country. Each of them usually contained one or more weak women. If someone else paid the bills and protected them from the big, bad world, such women generally played subservient roles throughout their lifetimes. I call those women "Cowboy Concubines." Ruby Lois Stewart Snow Holder Tomlinson, my grandmother. Circa 1953, age forty-one.

danced. More importantly, she liked to fuck. She got lots of chances to accomplish that activity. A steady stream of soldiers, sailors, and marines passed through Lita's home.

Lita found equal reason to be dazzled by the Kansas cowboy who arrived unexpectedly at her front door. I have repeatedly heard women say he was the best-looking man they ever saw. Lots of them believed MT looked like actor Robert Mitchum. They chased that sentiment with a harsh punch line: Robert Mitchum resembled an inferior version of MT.

But MT's appeal went beyond mere physical appearance. He was gifted with an incredible mind. A gift for numbers. He also had a photographic memory. His knowledge was encyclopedic. He was charming and witty.

MT's attributes were packed into a tall cowboy body that was hardened by a lifetime of hard work—an irresistible combination that appealed to women of all ages. Most women who met MT wanted to immediately chat him up, hug him, or fuck him. Many of them wanted to fuck him again after they discovered he had an eight-inch dick and a lot of enthusiasm.

MT and Lita made an incredible sexual duo. It was the stuff of movies. The best-looking girl anyone had ever seen hooked up with a man of like kind. They fucked like rabbits. They fucked like monkeys. They fucked in cars, on creek banks, and under apricot trees. That tsunami of sexual activity occurred before the birth control pill was invented. It's not difficult to guess what happened next—Lita got pregnant. The world came crashing down on her shoulders.

Lita was an unmarried, pregnant, gravely impoverished, sixteen-year-old white trash Indian girl who was living in a bordello. She knew that place did not provide much of a support structure. In

MT Liggett was a perfect model for the stereotypical American cowboy. MT made a big noise when he rode in, but always rode out when he was needed most. He left a trail of broken hearts, forgotten promises, and dirty diapers in his wake. MT was proud that he created about twenty-seven "love children" (bastards). I have found no evidence that he supported any of them except me and my half-brother Jim. The Old West and its cowboy heroes don't appeal much to a lonely child who hasn't eaten in three days. July 1949.

◇◇◇

Lita Snow with cowboy number one, MT Liggett. Campbell, California. July 21, 1949.

Lita's mind, it got worse from there. MT had only been in her life for a couple of months. She barely knew the man. The slim knowledge she possessed about him was not entirely favorable. Lita knew that MT looked like a god. When she first met him, that was very appealing. But masculine looks didn't hold much weight when she was doubled over with morning sickness.

Lita also knew that MT had a horrible temper, and was abusive, and unfaithful. It got even worse from there. Lita had been around sailors for years. When they came into her family's life, they made big noises. Everybody, especially the women, had a rip-roaring good time.

Then one inevitable day, the sailor showed up at the house, twisting his cute little white hat in his hands, crying, "I'm sorry. I'm being transferred. I have to get back to the base by morning." The sailor demanded a last party to celebrate the fun and money he brought to his paramour and her family. The sailor eventually got the woman off by herself. That was a big deal in those days. Most women were not free with their sexual favors. There was a darned good chance that she had not slept with the sailor. But this was his last night in town. He made promises. She wanted to set the hook. The seaman left her with his semen. The happy new couple partied until the last wild moment.

A father or brother drove them back to the navy base. Everyone laughed with delight when the sailor barely made it into the main gate before curfew. The group proudly exclaimed, "We fooled them ol' navy policemen, didn't we?" Ha! Ha! Laughs all around! The girl got into the car with her relative. She cried all the way home. Her empty room became a lonely prison when she closed the door.

Lita had seen endless variations of that theme play out with the women she knew. Sailors were good at soothing female loneliness.

But they always left you alone, in the end. Sometimes the guy came back; sometimes he didn't. Sailors made big promises. Most of them found another woman in the next port.

Lita was in a terrible fix. She had just begun to learn that life could be sweet and fun. She knew the growing mass of cells in her uterus was a ticking time bomb. It held the power to blow her happiness apart. She had to do something. But what?

Lita didn't have a chance to decide. MT's old sailor friend Tommy Tomlinson made Lita's first decision. He knew about sailors and the "next port syndrome." Tommy told MT to marry Lita—now.

Campbell City Hall was only a couple of blocks away from the bordello. My parents got married on November 8, 1949. The ceremony took about three minutes. A somber, abbreviated party finished off MT and Lita's wedding day. The attendees had to get up early for work in a few hours.

Lita and MT moved into a decrepit old camping trailer that was parked in the backyard of the bordello where they met. The new couple paid a steep rent for the trailer. The money went to Tommy Tomlinson. "Nobody gets a free ride in my house" was one of his favorite refrains.

The trailer was cramped and run-down. It made rough living for the new couple. But the trailer provided separation from the main house. It afforded them a little privacy.

Lita's next decision was made by others too. She got kicked out of high school. The official transcript indicates that Lita withdrew from school on November 27, 1949. The attached note stated she was going "to Kansas." That was bullshit. Everybody at school knew the truth: Lita got kicked out of Campbell High School because she was pregnant and married. That's the way

◇◇◇

Lita and MT moved into a decrepit old camping
trailer that was parked in the backyard of the bordello
where they met. Note Lita's tiny baby bump; that's
me. Campbell, California. Late winter, 1949.

school administrators handled pregnant students in those days. You couldn't have a pregnant Indian running around showing "fertile Myrtle" Croatian girls how to make babies. That shit might be contagious.

One day, Lita was the high-scoring captain of the basketball team and head majorette for the marching band. The next day, she was called to the principal's office. Lita became The Girl Who Never Came Back. But Lita didn't care. She didn't see much future in school anyway. Lita wanted to work full-time, fuck, and party.

Five months after Lita got expelled from school, a bizarre event occurred. It provided a cynical footnote to the demise of her educational prospects at Campbell High School. The school band always marched in the local Founder's Day parade. That was the most important event on the local civic calendar. The new lead majorette got sick. She couldn't march in the Founder's Day parade. The band director contacted Lita. He asked her to fill in as head majorette. Ever the worker, ever the pleaser, Lita accepted the band director's offer.

My soon-to-be mother was more than six months pregnant when she stuffed herself into the skimpy majorette's uniform. Lita said, "You couldn't even tell I was pregnant. I looked like a movie star." Everyone said she was the prettiest girl in the parade.

Lita told me she gave her best performance that day. She moved liked a ballerina. But no ballerina ever threw a baton like Lita. It looped and spun like a demented airplane propeller. People said she could throw the baton twenty feet in the air and catch it behind her back.

Lita told me that story many times. She was quite proud of her performance at the 1950 Campbell, California, Founder's Day parade. It was the pinnacle of her high school experience.

Lita was too deluded to see the hook in the worm. The pregnancy-forced expulsion thrust her into a life of second-class jobs. But the assholes at Campbell High School suffered no qualms about asking Lita to do a last job for them. It was cynical.

There was no operational reason for Lita to be out in front of the band. She didn't lead the players. Somebody else did that. Bands march every day without majorettes or drum majors. Those people make bands look classy. Lita added a level of sex appeal to what would otherwise have been a bland occasion. The public display of female flesh was rare in those days. Any way you cut it, the result was the same: the people at Campbell High School wanted to get a final look at Lita's magnificent body before they committed her to the dustbin of old memory and sub-par jobs.

Lita didn't know it, but she was living out an old family tradition. The white men at Campbell High School used the little Indian girl for quasi-sexual purposes, then threw her away. Hypocrites will always be with us.

Lita and MT Liggett lived together for just a few months. That was enough to lay the foundation for a pair of sick trends that haunted me for the next sixty-three years.

The first of those trends concerned Lita's housing choices. She bounced from apartment to apartment with stunning rapidity. Between times, Lita stayed in her mother's house. Occasionally she lived with MT. Back and forth she went. It was the ol' Lita two-step. She had a ready excuse for her behavior: "I was married to a low-ranking sailor. Those guys got transferred a lot."

But that was a smoke screen. Lita looked at her moves from a pragmatic standpoint. When my mother lived with Tommy Tomlinson, she was forced to give him 100 percent of her pay. I'm not

Lita's sports letter blocks from middle school and two-plus years of high school. She was high-scoring captain of the girls' basketball team. Lita said, "I ran right between the other girls' legs and stole the ball. They couldn't stop me when I ran for the goal." That was quite an accomplishment for a sophomore/junior girl who worked full-time away from school and lived in a bordello.

◇◇◇

This glove is the only remaining portion of Lita's majorette uniform. She showed me this painful artifact one time, glared angrily, and shoved it back into its hiding place.

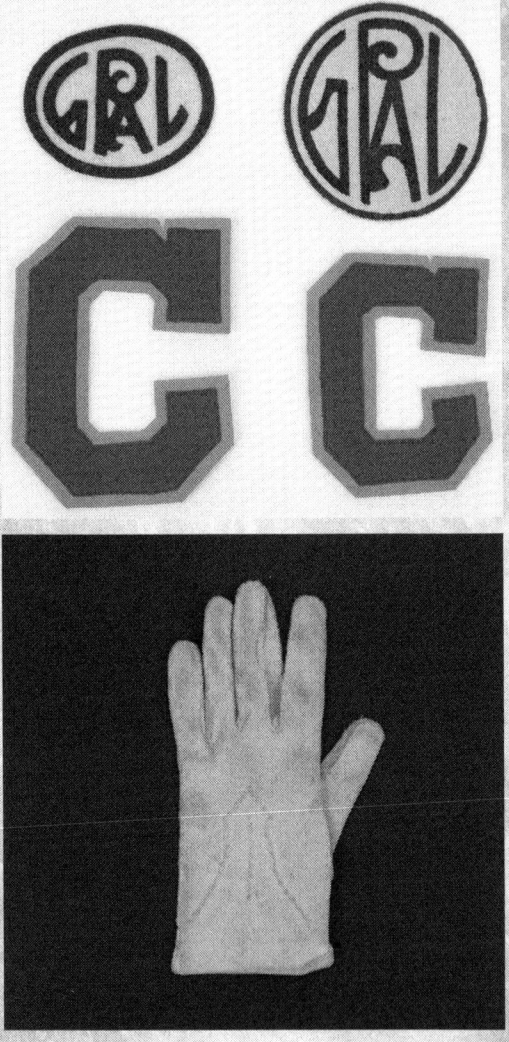

exaggerating; she gave him all of it. She had to beg for the return of a tiny portion of her own money to buy things she needed for herself and me. That gave Tommy Tomlinson unlimited power over Lita.

When my mother lived on her own, she didn't have to pay Tommy Tomlinson. He lost his power over her. When Lita lived in her mother's home, she did a long list of domestic chores. She accomplished these under the unerring gaze and harsh invective of two generations of angry women and a power-hungry sailor. When Lita lived elsewhere, she was free of her mother's endless list of chores. Those considerations were enough to make Lita work and live on her own.

The Santa Clara Valley was full of affordable housing choices in 1950. Lita had plenty of money to live a decent but Spartan life—if she counted her pennies. That wasn't difficult for her; she received her financial training from Tommy Tomlinson. She knew what was important. In Lita's mind, money that was spent on rent, food, and babysitters was wasted. It should have been spent on clothes, parties, and cigarettes. She applied that lesson with chilling efficiency.

Lita died when I was sixty-three. A few days before her death, she told me a story that finally brought the circumstances of my childhood into focus. The story began innocently enough. Lita told me she learned to bake cakes while working in a Mountain View, California, bakery. Lita spoke briefly about the fine details of cake baking: how to get a good crumb, how to level the cake's top. But she quickly got to the main point of her story: Lita liked the people who ran the bakery. They loved her. Everybody loved Lita. She said, "The bakery job was perfect. It was just a few blocks from home. I could go home at lunch to visit you."

Lita's last story was quite revelatory. Before I heard its fine details, I never fully grasped an important detail about my childhood. You see, I was just a few weeks old when Lita began her bakery job. I always knew I spent most of my childhood alone. It was an inescapable fact. Lita's story made me realize that sick behavior began much earlier than I previously thought. It is the harbinger of the lifelong neglect my mother visited upon me. Thus was wrought the second hideous trend of my childhood.

Over the years, I repeatedly heard Lita tell others about her bakery job. It is just one of many tales in the epic saga of Lita, the Valiant Woman Who Sacrificed All for Her Undeserving, Semi-Bastard Child. That shit played well with Lita's friends and family. But no one fully grasped what it was like to be in on my part of the deal. Imagine being an infant who spent uncounted hours in a dark, unheated apartment. I lacked food, water, or affection. I regularly spent at least four hours in a dirty, festering diaper.

I have no direct memory of that time, but Lita regularly reminded me about what had transpired. She wanted me to know how fortunate I was to have her as a mother. Year in, year out, Lita persisted in her narrative. Too bad she waited sixty-three-plus years to provide me with a semi-honest punch line.

Lita told me that she and MT agreed on very little during that period, but they found common cause about me; both indicated that I cried incessantly. MT elaborated on that concept: "You cried more than any baby I ever saw." Considering the circumstances, who wouldn't cry? Most of the time, I was locked away in a dark, quiet room, all alone. That was the good part. At irregular intervals, my solitude was punctuated by the screams of Lita and MT. Lita told me they yelled at each other all the time. This inevitably caused me to start crying.

⋄⋄⋄

When this photo was taken, I was spending uncounted
hours abandoned in a dark, unventilated apartment
(Lita closed the windows so neighbors couldn't hear my
screams.). Myron Thomas Liggett Junior, age about two
months; daddy's little cowboy, all dressed for the part.
Note the toy gun; they were getting me ready for the
Vietnam War, though they didn't know it at the time.

My cries gave MT a valid excuse to complete his anger. Lita said he screamed the same phrase at me over and again, "Shut up, shut up, shut up!" That course inevitably failed. My persistent screams angered MT more. Lita said he repeatedly swung his clenched fist down at my face and pulled his punches at the last moment.

"But I never saw him actually hit you," she told me. "I wouldn't have allowed that." Lita always added that last detail to the story. It made her look good to me and other people.

When I was young, that trite punch line offered consolation to what would have otherwise been a sad story. The experience of years has allowed me to finally ask a rhetorical question: What did MT do to me when you weren't around, Lita?

I cannot remember anything about the early imprinting I received from MT and Lita. But I'm certain that it made an impact upon my developing psyche. Any way you cut it, those times introduced the prime concept of my childhood: I learned to depend upon my own resources to provide what I needed. Some of those needs were basic. Like maternal love and food.

I'd like for you, my readers, to think back on your own early years. What is the first sentence you recall your mother saying to you? It's easy for me. I remember hearing that seminal phrase when I was two. Some folks believe that is too early to remember anything. I counter that it's hard to forget a raging force that is screaming, "You ruined my life by being born!" That's one heck of a revelation for anyone to absorb. But there's a funny aspect to that moment; I didn't find the gist of Lita's words to be exceptionally distressing. That makes me believe I heard them many times before.

I received independent corroboration concerning the validity of Lita's oft-spoken phrase from everyone in my family. They made it clear that my arrival added an unwanted complication to the whole family. From the day of my birth to the day that she died, my grandmother regularly advised me, "I didn't need another shit-assed little boy to care for."

I knew I had messed up by being born. It was a known fact. Viewed from my perspective, that flawed dynamic isn't as bad as it might seem. That is because I didn't really understand that Lita was my mother. I knew that she was my birth mother, but that biological fact didn't mean very much when applied to the operational details of my early life.

When I was quite young, Lita provided the rhythm for my life. You know, the drumbeat that sets a musical pace. But the melody was being carried by Lita's mother, Ruby, and her children. During my first four years, Lita and I lived with Ruby and her family about 75 percent of the time. I lived with six of Ruby's minor children. I am two years younger than her last child. My aunts and uncles were like siblings to me. They called Ruby Momma. So did I. That wasn't much of a stretch. Ruby provided more of a mothering influence than Lita. I was told ten thousand times over the course of my life that I was Momma's last child.

Ruby's family called my mother Loeta or Lita. I emulated them in that behavior too. Lita blended in with her siblings. She got lost in their crowd. It was a great crowd.

Other factors were involved in the devaluation of Lita's status as a mother. Hunger was one of them. My grandmother's family had lots of mouths to feed. There was a shortage of people in our home who could or would bring home the bacon. That put more pressure on Lita. She continued to work long hours away from home.

Back home in Oklahoma, my part-Cherokee Indian grandfather Cleve Snow was a sharecropper, fur trapper, and unprofitable maker of moonshine whiskey. Cleve said, "I only sold enough whiskey to buy sugar to make another batch. I drank the rest." When Cleve moved to California, he became the most sought-after Caterpillar tractor operator in the lower San Joaquin Valley—when he was sober. Most of the time he wasn't. When Cleve got drunk, he started violent bar fights. Broken long-neck beer bottles were his weapon of choice. Cleve burned down two low-rent hotels in Bakersfield, California, because he liked to smoke in bed. When no hotel would take him, Cleve passed out on a railroad track. The loss of his right foot slowed Cleve down a mite.

◇◇◇

My grandfather Cleve Snow (at right) and an unidentified inmate at a county jail farm. Cleve spent more time in that place than at home. He plowed county fields when that work was available. Cleve's jailers frequently sent him out alone with a sack of traps and a .22-caliber rifle so he could kill fur-bearing animals. It was impossible for my grandmother to depend on a man who spent most of his time drunk or in jail. Ruby moved to a Campbell, California, bordello. She took her mother and six minor children along for the hellish ride.

Housework was another factor that prevented Lita from taking an active role in my early life. When Lita lived in Ruby's house, she spent her time cooking, baking, or cleaning. When Lita wasn't working, she was away from home, having fun with men.

From the moment I was born, the die of all possible childhood futures had already been cast for me. My life revolved around Lita's jobs, housework, partying, and men. I was quite young when I reached an inescapable conclusion: Anything I requested from Lita deducted something from her other activities. I knew that any care I received from her would be brusquely and reluctantly given.

Not long after I was born, MT was transferred to another station. He promised to be faithful to Lita. He said he would "send all of his check home to you and my son." That didn't happen. MT lived a sailor's dream. He had a girl in every port. MT didn't send money home. He spent it on cheap Japanese whiskey and any woman he could get.

MT's letters to Lita were full of hearts and flowers. His letters to his twin brother, Byron, were full of male braggadocio ("I goddamn sure ain't an angel. I'll bet I have fucked 50 women since we got married.") and tales of drunken brawls and squandered pay and lists of the women he fucked.

Lita got her hands on the letters MT sent to his brother. They gave her the excuse she needed to formally separate from him. But he refused to give her a divorce. He refused to pay child support. The navy finally forced MT to send a small monthly allotment to Lita. He escaped that obligation when he separated from the navy and disappeared.

The financial aspect of MT's flakiness bothered Lita more than his infinite infidelities. She was a hard-working girl. She worked long hours, both at home and at her various jobs. Lita was sick of being poor. She wanted to wear nice clothes. She wanted to go out dancing two or three times a week. She wanted to eat and drink in nice places. She wanted to get bred, well and often. Those activities required money. Money that MT wasn't sending. Lita began to look to other sources for money and male consolation.

2

MOVES: SEXUAL AND OTHERWISE

When MT disappeared, he left my mother with two things. The first of those is obvious: me. A needy infant. But MT left my mother with something that was less obvious: a love of big dicks. The ol' grand salami. The burning desire to be the recipient of advanced cervical massage techniques.

Some of you might wonder why I have revealed these fine details to you. Because Lita's need for certain forms of sexual gratification drove her to the wrong men. Men who were bad for her and disastrous for me.

Lita began to date cowboy number two while she was still married to MT. He drove Lita across three states to visit MT at a navy base. They took the long, slow route and posed for smokin'-hot romantic photos together. Lita kissed her traveling companion at the navy station gate. About sixty seconds later, she met MT and gave him a passionate kiss. They got reacquainted in the sailor's way—holed up in a cheap hotel for twenty-four hours. MT told me, "We made the walls shake with our noise. We almost got kicked out of the place."

Lita walked MT back to the navy station gate. She gave him a last, passionate kiss. A passing shore patrolman cried out, "Move your ass inside, sailor. You're gonna miss formation."

Lita cried and waved her handkerchief as MT sprinted through the gate. She turned and walked down the block. Cowboy number two was leaning against his maroon Mercury coupe, smoking a cigarette. He looked up when Lita called out, "Hey, handsome, how ya doin'?"

Cowboy number two tossed his cigarette into the gutter and ran to Lita. He wrapped her in a passionate embrace and said, "My god, twenty-four hours felt like twenty-four years. I was going crazy thinking about you with him."

Lita knew how to handle a statement like that. "Hey, Romeo. The guy ain't gonna send me an allotment if I don't keep him interested. Relax. He's on ship for a long time. Besides, you've got me all the way home."

Lita and cowboy number two drove from Bremerton, Washington, to San Jose, California. It was a seven-day trip. They took lots of romantic photographs. They ate in fancy restaurants. Danced every night. Stayed in nice hotels. They made the walls shake in the hotels. They almost got kicked out of several places.

Too bad cowboy number two didn't know that Lita was plying him with formulaic passion. Canned heat. Lita was using her twat to get what she wanted: a money-seeking trip to see MT. She also got to have an all-expenses-paid, high-tone vacation. It was paid for by her sucker du jour. Cowboy number two lasted only about a year with Lita.

Lita cycled through men and apartments with incredible rapidity. She changed men because she could. She changed apartments to escape the attentions of former lovers. The first time

Lita began to date cowboy number two while she was still married to MT. But Lita couldn't pretend forever; he didn't meet Lita's sexual requirements; he wasn't big enough.

an old lover showed up on Lita's doorstep, she moved. Instantly. Within thirty minutes.

Lita knew how she wanted to live, even when she was fifteen. She worked hard in the potato shed all day, then drank, danced, and fucked the night away. Lita liked pretty men. She liked 'em tall, lean, and well hung.

When Lita dumped a man, she inevitably went out with someone else a few hours later. I know this is true because she took me along on many dates. She seemed to believe that each of these new men was going to be "the perfect father for Tommy." That was bullshit. Lita was lying to everyone—especially herself. She strung these guys along because she needed a sap to pay for a top-notch night on the town, then properly fuck her afterward.

MT was away at sea in a war zone for almost a year. In 1951, MT's letters revealed his ship was returning to San Diego. MT couldn't wait to get his hands on Lita's luscious little body. Lita apparently couldn't wait to get her hands on MT; she quit her job, dumped me with her mother, and raced to San Diego. Things didn't work out as the ardent couple had planned; MT ran off with a strange woman and left Lita stranded; or so he thought. Lita instantly found someone else to take her dancing.

I was raised on tales of the Valiant Lita, the Woman who Sacrificed All to Care for Her Undeserving, Unwanted, Semi-bastard Child. I willingly accepted the blame for that construct until I was sixty-two; then I found Lita's photographs. That fine collection contains lots of pictures of Lita dressed to kill. While she was the prettiest, best-dressed girl in every group, or photograph, until the waning years of her life, no one knew about a starving little boy sitting alone in various unheated ghetto apartments, dreaming about food, kitty cats, and the gardens he'd like to grow.

I gravitated toward anything and anyone who offered me the tiniest shred of love and affection, like this poor cat. I knew what I held in the moment was all I was going to get, most of the time.

◇◇◇

I only saw this photo and its unincluded companions once. Lita snatched the photo out of my hand when she saw me pick it up. When I asked about the wedding dress and unknown guy, she angrily told me to "mind your own fuckin' business."

This June 1951 photo is an early indicator of a lifelong tendency; Lita loved to pose for erotic photographs. She also loved risqué play. This photo also proves that a whore's life can be a lot of fun. My grandmother Ruby is the smiling woman who is leaning out the passenger door between Lita and the man. Most grandmothers of that era would have been outraged by the raunchy behavior that was occurring in front of their eyes. Not Ruby. She was willing to raise her children in a bordello because it provided the easiest way out of a fix. A final thought: Lita and my grandmother were my principal caregivers, yet both of them are in this photo, all dressed up to go out partying. Where was little Tommy Liggett, aged eleven months? Odds are, I was in a sweltering apartment, hungry and alone, wearing a rotten diaper.

◇◇◇

You sure as heck can't tell that Lita had given birth to a child a few months before this photograph was taken. She is draped over that chair like a Siamese cat in heat. MT sent her the silk underwear from Japan. Lita said, "I'd of rather had a larger fuckin' allotment check than a bunch of chink shit that didn't fit me right, anyway." Oh, Lita, this photo doesn't reveal the best part; you wore this outfit for other men to get even with MT.

◇◇◇

Lita wearing another piece of the silk lingerie ensemble MT sent from Japan. The enraptured-looking man is Tommy Tomlinson, Lita's stepfather. Lita said; "When I was younger, he tried to mess with me and all the other young girls, but I set him straight. I told him I wasn't going to have any of that shit." What about the other girls, Lita?

●━━━━━●

Lita was the most uninhibited person I ever met. She reveled
in the power of her body. Photo taken in the horse stalls
along Los Gatos Creek, Campbell, California, 1951.

◇◇◇

This is my favorite photograph of Lita. Why? Because it captures much
that was important to her. First among those attributes is the love of
the earth that was pivotal to Cherokee/Choctaw women. Note that Lita
is watering the lawn with a hose. No one else in our house full of lazy
women was willing to accomplish that life-bettering task. Lita said,
"When we first moved into that shithole, there was no lawn. I used to
sweep the dirt, just to make the place look a little better. Then I figured
out that if I watered the dirt, grass would come up." You did a good job,
Lita, the grass in the photo looks pretty lush. Then again so do you,
with your shorts rolled up and your hair too. The hair part is important;
it means that you had a date, later on. Also note the little dark dots
of nail polish on her perfect great toes. Lita kept her nails in perfect
condition, right until the day she died. Campbell, California, 1951.

◇◇◇

This was a racy photo for 1953; women didn't publicly display their pubic
mounds and pointy little nipples. Was Lita behaving like a sexual tiger,
building her self-esteem, or advertising? I believe she was doing all three.

◇◇◇

Lita was an Indian witch-woman. She knew how to cast effective
curses—like the one that is embedded in this photo; do you
see the crease? That's where Lita folded the photo in half,
then straightened it. In Lita's mind, that destroyed the bond of
love between her and the curse's intended target: MT Liggett.
Lita's archives are littered with curses of various types.

◇◇◇

The San Jose Municipal Rose Garden was a special place
for Lita. When she was a young girl, she walked miles
from the Campbell, California, brothel to be alone with
the roses. Lita took me to the rose garden on my birthday,
every year. This was done to take a commemorative
photo, to celebrate that things were better now. This
photo was taken on my second birthday. The poor guy was
the sap of the season. Look at the easy smile on his face;
the guy truly liked Lita and me. I never found another
San Jose Municipal Rose Garden photo that depicted
any of this sap's successors. None of those assholes cared
enough about Lita and me to commemorate anything.

MRS. M. T. LIGGETT
444½ VIEW STREET
MOUNTAIN VIEW
CALIFORNIA

◇◇◇

The real Lita, revealed. MT was launching fighter jets
in a war zone on the USS *Bonhomme Richard*, Lita was
at home, cashing MT's allotment checks and using the
envelopes to blot her lips before she went out with other
men and blotted her lips on various parts of their anatomy.
Among all the people in the world, only I knew Lita
well enough to recognize this envelope for what it is: a
curse. Lita was pissed at MT for not writing more often
and for not sending a larger portion of his navy pay.

Photographs from that era reveal that my mother went on group dates with three or four men. All of them were vying for her attention. Photographs and letters reveal she was sleeping with all of them. Alum Rock Park, San Jose, California, July 30, 1949.

◇◇◇

Lita regularly took photos of me with her boyfriends in this backyard spot. Note the shy expression on my face. I seem to be saying, rescue me from another strange guy who says he wants to be my daddy. In this case, he really was my daddy. Lita, MT, and me, first photo together since I was a few weeks old. Mountain View, California, 1952.

Things changed when cowboy number three rolled into Lita's life. Frank McMillan refused to go on Lita's group dates. He wanted her all to himself. Frank also wanted to screw every woman he met at cowboy bars. Since he went to bars every night, he screwed a lot of women. Frank McMillan was in pig heaven. Lita was furious. She and Frank fought incessantly. Lita was not happy with his philandering ways. Mostly though, she was unhappy about the obscene quantity of money Frank spent at his favorite watering holes. Bars and bar flies are expensive habits.

Lita worked more and more hours to get the rent money. Most of that overtime was accomplished on the night shift. That played into Frank's hands because when Lita worked long hours, Frank partied harder. It was a vicious cycle.

Frank and Lita separated and reconciled many times. There was no stability in our lives. Everybody was off-balance. Lita was wrapped up in her own problems. She was oblivious to mine. Lita didn't know that Frank was going to the bar every night. She didn't know that I wasn't eating dinner, most nights. She also didn't know I regularly spent six days without seeing another person in our apartment. Lita didn't give a shit. Truth be told, neither did I.

If Lita had ever asked me about my periodic bouts of solitary confinement, I would have provided a surprising answer: Isolation provided the lesser of two evils. Why? Because it was worse when Frank came home from the bar and found me alone. He snatched me off the floor pallet where I would sleep and repeatedly smashed me into a wall. No, Lita didn't know about any of that.

But Lita did know that I was failing in school. I didn't learn how to count and read until I was seven. She brushed off that problem with a comment, "You must be an idiot-child. Ain't

◇◇◇

I seem to be saying, here's another strange guy who
says he wants to be my daddy, so I won't take him
seriously either. Oh, Tommy, this first photo with Frank
McMillan reveals too much; he hated your childish
expression and was determined to wipe it off your face.
He did. Mountain View, California, September 1953.

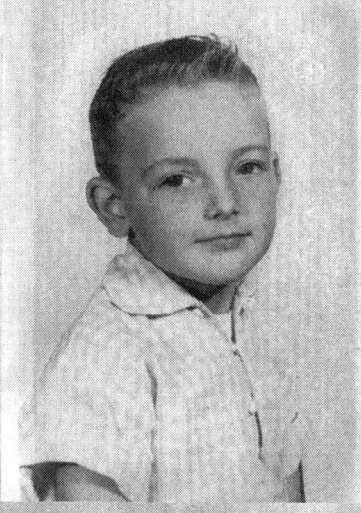

A 1954 telegram from Frank to Lita after she kicked him out, yet again. She was deathly ill, recovering from major surgery, and Frank was halfway across the country, begging for money. Oh, I left something out; Lita was on welfare and paying off the pair of loans Frank demanded she get for his benefit. What a guy.

◇◇◇

What kind of monster could starve, beat, belittle, brainwash, and wall-slam this four-year-old face? The Frank McMillan kind.

nobody in my family ever been that way. You must have gotten it from MT's side."

My first-grade teacher told Lita, "If you don't join the Parent-Teacher Association, I won't teach your child." Lita told that woman to "go fuck yourself" and stormed out of the room. Early the next day, my teacher made good on her promise. She moved my desk to the far end of the room, away from the other students.

For most of a school year, my teacher refused to acknowledge or speak to me. Any communication I received from her came in the form of a rebuke, scolding, or humiliating critique. The result was predictable; I forgot how to read and write. Thus began the nine-year span wherein it was widely believed that I was developmentally disabled. Lita was humiliated by the prospect that she had borne an idiot-child. Frank was determined to beat and work the stupid out of me.

Frank McMillan found a way to make this horrid stew a little richer. He liked to move—a lot. Apartment to apartment. City to city. State to state. At one point, we lived in three houses in six weeks. Frank didn't mind that sort of behavior. He claimed to have a minimalist view of life and personal possessions. He was a sort of cowboy Buddhist (but without the Buddha part).

Frank's real reasoning for our frequent moves was far more cynical; he didn't want anyone to know how we lived. As soon as someone began to see what was going on in the McMillan household, Frank moved. Lita and Frank's behavior caused me to live in more than twenty homes, rooming houses, and apartments before I was eleven years old. I attended eight schools before I was eleven.

Lita and Frank forced me to feed and entertain myself. That last part had a plus side. When the sun was shining, I played alone in my garden. When the sun went down, I retreated inside

DeARSANTA
I hAVe beeN A LiTTLe
biT good AND A LiTTLe
biT bAD.

HAS iT beeN SNOWing
wHere you A re?
HAS ANy oF your
raIN DEer beeN siCK?
I wouLD LiKe A TooL
KiT A TraIN, AND
buiLDing bLoCKS.
Love Tommy

◇◇◇

I wrote this note to Santa Claus when I was four.
It indicates that I was knowledgeable in the basic
fundamentals of reading and writing. I also knew how to
count to ten in both English and Spanish. Counting was
easier for me in Spanish, because I learned from the other
kids I met in the fields and fruit processing sheds. (I was
typically the only white child in the group.) Two years
after I wrote this note, I forgot how to read and write.

Frank McMillan, drunk and pissed off on moving day. Frank
said, "I don't want to own anything I can't throw in a car in
thirty minutes and git gone." Substitute the word saddlebag
for car in the last sentence, and Frank could have been
describing himself as a nineteenth-century Texas cowboy.

◇◇◇

A young recruit being put through the paces by his marine-
trained drill sergeant. Frank is ensuring that I get into his
car quickly, quietly, and without tracking a bunch of dirt
onto the seat. Note my nut-brown skin and bare feet. I was
the king of orchards, creek bottoms, fields, abandoned
lots, and hobo camps. My subjects were semi-tame pigeons,
stray cats, and starving dogs. I ran wild as a deer because
there was nothing and no one waiting for me at home.
Photo taken in Lost Hills, California, during the second
of our numerous breakneck road trips to Texas, 1955.

My cousin Larry Daniels, age five, and me at age eleven (right). Circa 1961. Larry's parents rented a semi-derelict farm house that was lost in the middle of a shabby Santa Clara, California, trailer park. My grandmother's Spartan trailer was parked next door.

◇◇◇

Three hours before this photo was taken, I didn't know MT Liggett existed. He filled me with child-sized dreams of familial love and new bicycles, then was gone in another three hours. I didn't see MT for seven years. This perfectly framed photograph was all smoke and mirrors, like most things with Lita and her men.

our shabby apartment. I read books, magazines, and any written work that passed within my field of vision—child, adult, modern, ancient, or erotic. When I was especially bored, I read through large portions of the Encyclopedia Britannica. My eight-year-old brain didn't understand most of what I read in advanced texts, but the words provided a human touch to my life. The pages said to me that there are people in the world—you are not alone.

I was sexualized and resexualized by my mother, by relatives and friends. Male relatives provided me with erotic magazines. My mother tried to make me touch her pussy when I was five. I witnessed my mother having sex many times. Neighbor boys tried to suck my dick when I was six. Male relatives introduced me to the joys of mutual masturbation when I was seven. I was molested by an older boy at the age of nine, but still had not yet experienced an orgasm. Damn!

What you have read thus far is a brief synopsis of my creation and the first ten years of my life. It is introductory material. The stage is set. Enjoy the rest of the tale. As *Hee Haw*'s David "Stringbean" Akeman famously said, "Hang on, children."

3

AMERICAN DREAMS BUILT
ON PILLARS OF SMOKE

Frank and Lita's marriage was on the rocks. They needed to find a way to cement the bonds of their relationship. You know, a magic bullet that cured all their problems, one that wouldn't require Frank to stay home at night, or made him stop fucking other women, or spending 110 percent of the family income.

They tried to have a baby but gave up after a third pregnancy almost killed Lita.

Frank and Lita tried another tack; they decided to buy a house. They wanted to bind themselves together with a web of mortgage debt that would stand in proxy for the glaring lack of a co-produced baby. Their house-buying aspirations weren't surprising to me. Lita ranted at Frank all the time about money. She wanted him to be more frugal so they could buy investment property. Frank eventually discerned the salient points of Lita's argument. This came after a particularly nasty separate-and-then-make-up cycle. That event made Frank see the benefit of buying into Lita's home investment schemes.

He told anyone who would listen, "I'm a gonna build me up some equity. Make myself a real estate hotshot. Get me my big break." That was pure bullshit. Frank bought a home as a last-ditch effort. It was the only remaining avenue by which he could prevent his best piece of ass and all-round money-earner from walking out the door.

Frank and Lita began to look at houses. That process took months. Why? Because house-hunting in the 1950s and '60s San Jose was quite different than it is today. Modern home shoppers surf the net, then drive around to look at homes that are scattered across the valley. In 1960, we drove around to look at new cities. Everywhere we looked, massive housing developments had sprung up like mushrooms after a fall rainstorm.

Ah, but those new cities exacted a deadly toll on the landscape—and on me. I was a child of nature. Orchard, field, and stream were my domains. My day was spent seeking, harvesting, and memo-rizing interesting plants.

When I was three years old, I could identify every type of stone fruit tree. Leaves on, leaves off. I knew them all. I cherished Carpathian walnut and Royal Anne cherry trees that towered and spread eighty feet. They had trunks like oak trees. Each tree produced hundreds of pounds of superior-quality fruit. I watched in horror as puke-green World War II army-surplus bulldozers pushed the trees over and smashed them into fifty-foot-tall piles that were a hundred feet wide. Some of the trees still had ripe fruit on their branches. Dirt is best graded when the soil is dry in the summer. Fruit time.

I asked some of the destruction workers, "Why didn't you pick the fruit? Someone could have eaten that. Aren't you bothered by the waste?" The workers scoffed at my youthful ignorance and

◇◇◇

I found an oak-sized cherry plum tree growing in the front yard
of an abandoned house. I studiously watched the ripening fruit
until it was at the perfect stage for making plum preserves. Lita,
my grandmother, and I harvested enough of the plums to fill an
ancient clawfoot bathtub. Each piece of fruit had to be inspected,
cut, and chopped. From the age of six onward, I was Lita's little
fruit processor. When I had enough fruit for a batch, Lita said,
"Tommy, come stir the jam." I dragged a chair over to the stove,
stood on the seat, and stirred Lita's cheap enamel pot with a huge
wooden spoon. It was hard work. I had to use both hands. In Lita's
mind that was a symbolic act; she also stood on kitchen chairs to
do kitchen work when she was a wee child. Such were the ways in
which the baton of child slavery was passed from one generation
of my mother's family to the next. San Jose, California, July 1959.

said, "There ain't no time to harvest the fruit. The contract's due. A few tons of damned fruit ain't worth nowhere near what a crop of houses is."

Callous men poured high-sulfur diesel oil on the fleshy green foliage. Covered the delicious fruit. Soaked the hundred-year-old bark. The killers lit cigarettes, then threw the burning matches onto the fuel-soaked mountain. When they were sure the fire was burning hot, they walked away. They farted, told crude jokes, and wondered about their next job.

My family sometimes found occasion to drive up into the mountains that surround the Santa Clara Valley. We were drawn to the steep terrain and wildland beauty. We always stopped at several places on the long switchback grades. We got out of the car and looked down at the valley floor. I remember seeing pillars of smoke rise into the sky from various points around the valley—burning fruit trees. They were the funeral pyres of a vanishing way of life. They were the signal beacons that heralded the Santa Clara Valley's entrance to the modern world, to becoming Silicon Valley.

The fruit tree ashes smoldered for days. Their white remains were ground into the dirt. They became foundation markers for legions of cheap suburban houses.

Ah, mankind never seems to outgrow its youth. We are like children, always crying for new toys. My white relatives killed my Indian relatives to clear the way for a new way of life. They wiped two continents sparkling clean with a lily-white cloth. A hundred years later, new generations of white men killed off the now old American way of life to make way for another new one.

I call this behavior the Kleenex effect. When you want to cover a big ol' wet sneeze, a sheet of tissue is the most important thing in your life. After you blow your nose, the tissue goes into the trash, forever forgotten and never brought to mind.

What redeeming value can be found in a culture that demands something must die so something new can be built? Can't we build onto the old so that we can incorporate it into the new? That was a rhetorical question, folks. I was there. I already know the answer. The fruit trees were ritual sacrifice of the highest kind.

The development of my beloved valley went on and on. I watched shaded two-lane country crossroads become arterial intersections. Tacky strip malls replaced fruit trees on their corners. I was devastated. Everywhere I looked, things I loved were destroyed or changed. But it happened in bits and pieces, not all at one time. It was as if a massive ice cream scoop removed individual orchards and replaced them with houses.

A blob of house was laid down here, then another one there. Before long, heartbreaking beauty was replaced by cookie-cutter suburbia. A few orchards remained here and there, but they had the haggard look of condemned men standing on the gallows. They know they are alive in name alone.

Most people believe the malignant growth of modern San Jose was accidental, the result of market forces and demands. But it wasn't. It was driven by corrupt, greedy politicians who saw urban growth as a revenue stream. Much of the modern deforestation and development of the greater San Jose area was orchestrated by City Manager "Dutch" Hamann. That demon was raised in Orange County during the first great Southern California housing boom. He saw ugly suburban sprawl replace the finest citrus groves the world will ever see.

Dutch put his childhood imprinting to work when he moved to San Jose; he declared war on the nation of fruit trees. He did more than any other person to change the Santa Clara Valley from a tree-covered paradise into a miniature Los Angeles. The call, "Buy where Dutch buys," led countless insiders down the orchard path to ill-gotten riches.

It jarred my senses to ride down all-new streets that were lined with homes and shopping centers. The smelly black asphalt. The blinding white glare of new driveways and sidewalks. It was horrid.

Many builders added a cynical touch to their new homes. They left tractor-damaged, water-starved fruit trees in the bare-dirt yards of their tacky little ticky-tacky homes. The builders saw them as selling points. They told potential buyers they could "own a piece of valley history. Own your own fruit tree." I'm a fruit tree lover. I didn't see it that way. I thought it was like using Jewish gravestones for pavers in Nazi death camps.

In July 1960, Frank and Lita took me to see the unfinished building that would soon become our new home. I was not surprised when I discovered that place was built on the edge of a partially demolished prune orchard. I knew the field well. My family had picked strawberries there, seven years before.

I followed Lita and Frank into the house. They gave me the grand tour. Frank pointed to an open doorway and said, "That's gonna be your room, over there." I walked into my future room and looked around. A full-grown prune tree stood just outside the unfinished window opening. I reached through and touched the downy leaves. The branches were laden with immature fruit. I remember thinking that tree set a bumper crop of fruit, but no one will ever eat a bite. I also knew that it would be the worst kind of folly to fall in love with the tree. Surveyor's stakes indicated a stucco wall would stand in the tree's place when I returned.

I was just ten, but I found great symbolism in that moment. I

The front-most pair of cowboys in this photograph are looking at the foundation of Frank and Lita's uncompleted house. The smaller figure is me. I was confused by the view I found when I stared away from the house. My family picked strawberries on this once-lovely spot, seven years before. At that time, magnificent fruit trees stretched endlessly toward a green horizon. When this photo was taken, my vision was filled with mountainous piles of burning trees on one side, going up in pillars of smoke, and tacky new homes on the other. August 1960.

◇◇◇

1959. Any animal or human who had this gaze cast upon them would have reason to be very afraid. Frank McMillan (left), drunk and pissed at Big Basin State Park, 1959, with Johnny Crossland.

knew I was about to have my own room. That had happened only once before. I knew this home promised more stability than I had ever known. I was supposed to be happy with those eventualities, but I wasn't. I knew that fruit trees died to provide space for my room. I felt like a young Zeus, whose father was learning to savor the taste of his own children.

When Frank McMillan walked into his new home, he wasn't thinking about fruit trees. He was pleased that he had finally secured his own piece of the American dream. In that regard, Frank had a lot of help. He bought the home on Senter Road on the G.I. Bill. He paid for the closing costs and fees. No down payment. The monthly payments weren't much more than the rent on our shitty ghetto apartment. That's why everybody loved the rapacious development of the Santa Clara Valley. The buy-in for the sucker was cheap. But the dividends for the planet came dear.

I only saw the new house twice before we moved in. We spent just a few minutes in that place. That was time enough for Frank to burden me with a new form of abuse. Most people who know what I previously endured probably believe that Frank's existing suite of behaviors was sufficient to further his purposes. Oh, no. Frank McMillan was always willing to layer new abuses upon the old. They accumulated on my psyche like stray cats around my back door.

While Lita wandered around the inside of the house, Frank led me into the front yard. When we got there, he turned around and hit me with a whole new concept: "I work forty hours a week to make all of this possible. That's more than enough for one man to do. When I come home, I wanna put my feet up an' read the paper. You're gonna take care of the yard. All of it. Front and back. If I have to come out here an' pull a single weed, I ain't gonna be happy—an' neither are you."

Frank chased his speech with a look of pure, unadulterated malice. Harsh experience had taught me to pay more attention to Frank's facial expressions than his words. His words said, "I want for you to keep the yard nice and clean for me." His look said, "I'm gonna be watching you like a hawk and waiting for you to make a mistake. First time you make the tiniest mistake, I'm gonna fuck you up." That look was enough to make me damn near shit my pants.

I quickly nodded my head in assent. That wasn't enough for Frank. He barked, "Did you say something?"

I squeaked, "Yes, sir."

Frank roared, "Yes, sir, what?"

I said, "Yes, sir. I will keep the yard clean. You won't have to pull a single weed."

Frank spun on his heel and left me standing alone in the yard. But he spoke a chilling warning as he walked back into the house. "We'll see, won't we?" Welcome to the joys of home ownership, Tommy.

Frank's ill temper that day was driven by two factors. The first was most important; he was on the tail end of a weekend-long drunk. He wanted to curl up with a whiskey bottle and a good book, then pass out cold. Frank met any distraction that veered from that objective with anger. Like taking his wife to see her long-awaited dream home.

Then there was Frank's other reason to be angry. We were alone when he delivered his yard-care speech. Frank became a more comprehensive bully when he had me all to himself. That's when the real Frank McMillan came out. That was the man nobody else knew. When other people were around, Frank usually managed to temporarily shove most of his demons into their secret hiding places. You know, pretend he was a doting father, not a drunken marine-trained drill sergeant who hated little kids, especially me.

Our new home was only a few miles from our rented apartment. It was an easy move. The combination of whiskey-induced poverty and frequent residence changes allowed us few belongings. I didn't have my own room at our rented apartment. I slept on the floor. I didn't have a closet or dresser for my belongings. I lived out of boxes. Three small cardboard boxes, to be specific. I didn't have much stuff.

My part of the move was easy. Aside from the boxes, I brought a few rusty old garden tools and a hundred pounds of banana squash to the new house. I picked the squash from my backyard garden the day we moved. It was my first big crop, a milestone in my life as a gardener. Then I walked away from my garden of longest duration. Photos taken on that day reveal a happy boy, friends, and the produce from my first crop. But the photos don't reveal an important fact: Two minutes after the camera shutter clicked, I walked away from the garden and the friends.

We moved our things into the new house. It took all day to get settled. We went to bed early. Frank and Lita had an old but nice double bed. No one gave any thought to my sleeping arrangements. That was because, no matter where we lived, I always slept on the floor. Frank and Lita assumed that was where I would sleep in the new house. I must have thought the same thing, because I automatically made my pallet on the floor. I knew the drill. Fold a stolen army-surplus blanket in half. Place it on the floor. Spread a cotton sheet. Put a stolen gray navy blanket on top of the sheet. If the weather was very cold, my great-grandmother's quilt went on top of the pile. I had an old, thin pillow.

✧✧✧

This staged photo depicts me (on the left), the Perfect Robot Child on moving day, part twenty-something. I smiled and pretended I wasn't bothered by the loss of my garden and home of longest duration. I smiled and pretended I wasn't bothered by the loss of my only friend, Charles Reynolds (the older man in the center). I felt no loss about the prospect of not seeing the kid who was holding my squash. He was just someone I barely knew. San Jose, California, September 1960.

◇◇◇

The previous squash-bearing photo was staged in every aspect,
right down to its location, in my neighbor's perfect backyard.
I demanded that Lita also take photos in our backyard, in
the middle of my squash vines. I wanted a true memento of
my first big crop. This photograph is the money shot for
moving day—yet again. Note the grim expression on my face;
I am not happy, but I am quiet. I knew that complaining about
my lot would get me a sore ass that would last for days.

There was nothing new in that combination for me, or so I thought. Oh, Tommy. That was a bad assumption. The floors I previously slept on were made of wood. A few were covered with rank-smelling rugs. In my book, stinky rugs were okay because they were soft.

Our new floor was covered with vinyl-asbestos tile. It was laid on a solid concrete slab. That sonofabitch was hard. It was also stone cold, even in late summer.

A threadbare army blanket and sheet made a thin pad for a thinner boy. My little bones were no match for my new room's cement floor. I didn't sleep very well that first night. Because of that detail, I heard Frank and Lita loudly christening their new master suite. I could hear them going at it again, early the next morning. They never masked the sounds of their passion. Frank liked to trumpet his amorous accomplishments. Lita liked to titillate me.

Lita was bright and cheery at the breakfast table. New house. Good sex. Repeatedly. American dream stuff. What's not to like? Lita chirped endlessly about how good she felt. The house was perfect. She talked a lot about present and future window coverings.

Frank sipped from a pint bottle of whiskey and nodded his head at the right moments. Otherwise, he looked bored, grumpy, and hung over, like he wanted to be somewhere else.

I sat at the table and poked at my food. That was unusual for me. Food could be a scarce commodity in Frank and Lita's homes. When given the opportunity, I generally ate everything in sight except the tableware. But this meal was different. I was tired. My back was sore from sleeping on the concrete floor. I missed my garden back at our old rental. I missed the cracked sidewalks and stately old homes of downtown San Jose. I was grumpy.

Frank didn't like my expression. He knew that something was

up. He sneered out a question, "Why are you a sittin' there all pouty-faced, boy?"

I made big mistake; I revealed my true feelings to Frank. I didn't deliver the preprogrammed, submissive speech he expected to hear. I said, "The floor was hard and cold. I didn't sleep last night. I'm tired and my back hurts."

Oh, boy. Big fuckin' mistake, Tommy. You became the turd in the punch bowl. Lita broke down and cried. Frank went ballistic. Their housewarming after-glow flew right out the window.

The precise order and verbiage of the decidedly one-sided dialogue that followed my response do not bear repeating in this book. Frank pulled them from the tired, but spirited repertoire of sayings he had accumulated over the years. When Frank grew tired of yelling, he grabbed me by the back of my T-shirt and spun me around. He lifted me off the ground with his left hand and began to methodically kick my ass with his right foot. He carried me toward my new bedroom. Every step was punctuated with a new kick. Each kick was accompanied by his marine-drill-sergeant voice screaming one inch behind my ear.

When we got to the door, he swung me further with his left hand and caught me with the right. He rocked me backward, then strongly forward. Frank released his grip when I was at the end point of the arc. I flew through the door and across the room. My face smacked into the far wall. I slid down the wall and collapsed. I was stunned.

Frank stood in the doorway and ranted some more. I tried to crawl into the corner. I expected Frank to charge through the door at any moment and pick me up to slam me against the wall a few more times. I thought, stay loose, it'll hurt less. Just take it, it's gonna happen anyway.

This was Frank's preferred seating position at his kitchen table in the Senter Road house. He (on left) appears uncharacteristically happy in this photo. Then again, the prettiest girl in town just served him a brandy cordial in a cut crystal goblet, and Tommy is nowhere to be seen. With Kenneth Kirkley, Lita's sister Betty's husband, circa 1964.

But Frank didn't come into the room. Maybe he felt charitable that day. Or was it because Lita was just down the hall? Frank looked around my room and got a disgusted look on his face. He said, "Clean up this fuckin' mess."

I said, "Yes, sir," and leaped to my feet. I began to scurry around the room and shuffle the boxes that contained my possessions. Frank slammed the door and walked down the hall.

It took me only a few minutes to sort out my new room. I was finally able to relax. The rush of moving was over. Frank and Lita were down the hall, loudly having another round of sex. Lita was rewarding her man for disciplining her unruly child.

I looked at my surroundings and had a revelation. My room was stark, hard, and empty. It resembled a cell, the kind inhabited by monastic monks. The room was a solitary place, filled with quiet and penitence. I was sorry I had been born. I was sorry I caused so much trouble for Frank and Lita. So it went on that bright summer day. I didn't trust my new surroundings enough to make them my own. They were like all other aspects of my life— conditional and revocable. I knew better than to fall in love with any place. Tomorrow I might be in another.

4

GRASS GREEN PRISON WALLS

The company that built our home made a lot of noise about the free front lawn they provided to all buyers. That was a big deal in those innocent times. Everybody knew that lawns were expensive. What a deal!

I was excited. I knew all about growing fruit trees, jade plants, and banana squash, but lawns were unknown to me. I was going to learn how to grow something new.

The home building company called Lita and told her the free front lawn would be planted on a certain date. Frank told me to make sure I was there when the landscaping crew arrived. They needed someone from our family to sign a receipt for their work.

I parked myself in the front yard an hour before the lawn planting was scheduled to occur. Excitement aside, I didn't want to risk missing the lawn workers. Frank would have been livid. I waited and waited for the landscaping crew to arrive, but no trucks appeared on the horizon. I became impatient and restless.

I eventually heard a familiar sound in the distance. It came from a small Ford tractor. Most of the farmers I knew had one or more of the things. A tractor on the road wasn't an unusual sight in that place and time.

I was surprised when the little tractor pulled into our driveway. The operator shouted, "I'm here to plant your new lawn."

I shouted back, "Where is your work crew?"

He laughed. "You're lookin' at him."

Without further discussion, the man put the tractor in gear and drove onto our small front yard. He dropped the rear-mounted rippers just enough to disturb the top half inch of soil. The rippers looked like comb teeth passing through a crew cut. In five or six passes, the whole front yard was crosshatched with shallow lines that were about six inches apart.

The man parked the tractor in the driveway and retrieved a centrifugal seeder from the front bucket. That type of seeder was designed in the nineteenth century. One person could plant a ten-acre wheat field in just a couple of hours. The tractor man filled the seeder with grass seed. It took him ten seconds to sow our lawn.

The man dumped the remaining seed into a bag and filled the seeder with ammonium sulfate. I knew all about that type of fertilizer. It was valued by local farmers more for its sulfur content than as a fertilizer. Sulfur is an effective antidote for alkaline soil and water. The tractor man applied the fertilizer to the planted area. That took another ten seconds.

The tractor man dumped the excess fertilizer into a bag, put the seeder back into the tractor's front bucket, and retrieved a clipboard. I signed for the lawn. He tipped his hat to me and was gone. From introduction to farewell, he wasn't on our property more than five minutes.

Even a naïve little kid like me knew the whole "free lawn" thing was a scam. Frank knew it too. He fumed for days about the injustice of it all. In Frank's mind, it was just another example of big business taking advantage of the working man.

Our new lawn was planted. Everyone involved knew that it was a flawed installation. But that didn't matter to Frank; he expected our lawn to thrive. What am I saying? Frank expected it to be the best one on the block. It never occurred to Frank to emulate some of the other homeowners in our development; they abandoned the scamster's free lawns and planted better ones. That didn't happen. Why? Frank wasn't willing to move his ass long enough to do some work out in the yard.

Frank believed he worked hard enough Monday through Friday. Frank viewed his nights and weekends as rewards, just compensation for being a workaday hero. Doing yard work would have interfered with that fantasy. Which brings this little story back to its beginning. Frank expected a ten-year-old boy who had never grown a lawn to deal with one that was installed incorrectly. Great.

A love of reading saved my skinny ass a lot of pain. I memorized the handout that came with our house. It indicated that the new lawn had to be moist all the time. If not, the new grass seedlings would burn in the August sun.

I didn't mind my little watering cycle. Why? I love to watch plants grow. I also knew that if our flawed lawn didn't thrive, my butt would pay the toll. Frank reminded me of that possibility several times a day.

Against all odds, the lawn thrived. In about a month, it was six inches tall and as green as Ireland. That suited me fine. I like green. I continued to pour water and fertilizer onto the front yard. My not-spanked ass thanked my brain and hands for their diligence.

Frank watering our newly seeded lawn. It was close to 100
degrees F when the lawn received its flawed installation,
but Frank demanded I keep it moist, 24/7. That crucial
detail nailed my backside to our home for the rest of the
summer. Every half hour, I was outside with a hose, watering
the lawn. Frank's uncle, Arthur McMillan, is clowning
around in the top of the photograph. September 1960.

I'll never forget what happened next. It was Saturday. I woke in an empty house. I thought nothing about it; that was normal. I scrounged around for some food and walked outside to water the lawn. Frank drove up just as I reached to turn on the spigot. He barked at me through the car window, "Don't water the lawn. Put the hose away."

I quickly complied with the change of orders. The hose was in the garage in about two minutes, coiled in a manner that would have pleased any sailor.

Frank pulled his car into the driveway, got out, and said, "Come here." I followed him to the rear of his battered 1954 Chrysler New Yorker. A gasoline-powered lawn mower was sticking out of the trunk.

Frank lifted the heavy steel contraption like it was a toy and placed it on the ground. He pushed the mower into the garage and stopped. Frank showed me how to clean the air filter and change the oil. He rolled the mower outside and filled the tank with gasoline. Frank showed me how to start the engine. He killed the engine and said, "You start it."

I started the mower. I thought, this is great! I was laughing my ass off.

Frank killed the engine, looked me in the eye, and said, "If I ever have reason to start this sonofabitch again, I'll whip your lazy ass till you're too sore to walk. Do you believe me?"

"I believe you, sir."

Frank said, "Good. Now I'm gonna show you the right way to mow a lawn. I paid extra for a grass catcher. It'll make your job easier, not that your lazy ass deserves anything to be made easier than you already got it."

Alas, the grass catcher turned out to be dangerous and ineffective. It wouldn't stay attached to the mower. The clippings spewed everywhere except in the collection bag. Frank gave up after several abortive attempts to make the grass catcher function properly. He barked, "Fuck it," and ripped the catcher from the idling mower. The mower tipped over and began to rev wildly. The engine smoked, coughed, and stalled.

Frank calmly took a step back and spun the defective catcher away. It sailed across the lawn, sidewalk, mow strip, and the full width of Senter Road. The catcher finally landed and skittered on the steep shoulder and up the hill, leaving a bright green trail of grass clippings in its wake.

All that activity transpired in a few seconds, but it seemed to be an eternity. I was standing beside Frank, pretending to be invisible. That ploy sometimes worked. Come what may, I didn't want Frank to redirect his mower-derived anger toward me. That didn't happen, this time.

Frank calmly reached into the bib pocket of his overalls and pulled out a fresh plug of W. N. Tinsley chewing tobacco. Frank peeled the cellophane wrapper and took a big bite from the plug. He mechanically chewed the tobacco until he created a chaw. He pushed the chaw into his cheek with his tongue, then spit a long stream of tobacco juice onto the grass. Frank grinned at me and said, "The nicotine will kill the bugs."

Frank looked down at the overturned mower, then to the far side of the road. The grass catcher's freshly galvanized bottom was sparkling in the sun. Frank redirected to me and said, "That's all right with me. I wanted you to rake the lawn anyway. You finish mowing."

I pulled the grass-clogged mower back onto its wheels. I made several attempts to start the engine, but it was flooded with gasoline. I eventually got it going and began to mow, first one direction,

I made our lawn thrive, in spite of its flawed planting. Note that the lawn is weed-free and perfectly edged. Those jobs were done by hand. Note the Royal Family sweet peas in the flower bed on the right side of the photograph. I planted these for Lita, because she wanted to have cut flowers on her table. March 1961.

◇◇◇

I was proud of my sweet peas. March 1961.

then the other. Every bit was cut twice. Frank then showed me how to rake. He made sure I removed every speck of cut grass but didn't scour the tender roots. That was a more difficult task than using the mower. My frequent applications of water and fertilizer made the lawn grow like crazy.

I must have raked and removed 200 pounds of clippings that day. It took a long time. Frank watched my every move. He instantly barked out corrections when I applied too much or too little pressure to the rake. Frank had me right where he wanted—under his thumb. He loved to watch me do manual labor. Frank had sweated under the hot Texas sun when he was a child. He seldom missed an opportunity to make me do the same thing.

I can't say that I enjoyed the work I did that day. It was hot and difficult. But it was also gratifying. I told myself I was finally doing something that contributed to our household. I thought I was growing up.

A few weeks after we moved into our new home on Senter Road, Lita got a notice from my new school. All parents were expected to attend a mandatory orientation. Lita snorted and laughed when she read the school letter. "Ain't no fuckin' way I'm gonna miss a half-day's work because of that shit. You've been to lots of schools, Tommy. You'll figure it out for yourself."

I nodded my head in agreement. It was old hat for me.

For once, I was happy to see the first day of school arrive. Our new lawn's thirty-minute watering cycle had locked my butt at home all summer. I didn't get to explore our new neighborhood. I didn't meet any of the local children. I was just happy to escape from the fifty-by-one hundred-foot confines of Frank's house.

I first saw Hillsdale School when our bus pulled into the loading zone. It was a typical 1950s California school; lots of low, detached buildings were connected by covered breezeways. The place was a swirling sea of children. Many of them seemed to know each other. I knew no one. But that was normal for me. I was always the new kid everywhere I went.

Someone told me where to find the fourth-grade classrooms. I turned and followed the crowd that surged in that direction. I felt like a leaf caught in a riverine current. We were a few minutes early. Our classroom was not open.

The other kids were playing and joking around with each other. Most of the activity was centered around one boy. He was six inches taller than any other child in the yard, tall and blond. He was wearing a real buckskin jacket. The sleeves were trimmed with a four-inch fringe. The tall boy's every gesture indicated a proud awareness of his self-proclaimed superiority. He swaggered around the other kids like he was the cock of the walk.

A scrawny-looking Mexican kid stepped out of the crowd. Without preamble, he walked over to the tall boy and punched him in the jaw. It was a perfect right hook. The blow knocked the tall boy to the ground. He didn't seem to be hurt, but I could tell he was cowed by the short boy. The tall boy stayed on the ground. He looked up at his attacker but didn't do or say anything. I had seen lots of fights. Experience told me that the tall boy could get in a few punches before the teachers rushed in.

I ran over to the tall boy and said, "Why are you just lying there? You're bigger than him. Get up!"

The smaller boy was facing away from me, but when he heard me speak to the tall boy, he wheeled and said, "He won't hit me because I am Mr. A. He knows that if he beats me up, my brother, Mr. B, will come after him. If he beats that brother up, my next brother, Mr. C, will come after him. If he beats that brother up, he'll have to face the whole D gang."

The crowd of students that surrounded the action had been strangely quiet, until then. But when the smaller boy mentioned the familial name of the D gang, the other children emitted a collective "Ooh," and drew back a step. Why did they do that? Because the D family were very bad people. I was to receive echoes and warnings about that family's activities many times in the coming decades.

In one sense, there was nothing new about this turn of events. I had heard a lot about Mexican street gangs at my last school. One of my classmates regaled us with grisly stories. He spoke of a machete-caused murder he witnessed in reverent terms, as if he had just viewed a particularly interesting movie. But things were different at my new school. It was the first time I had ever been around someone who was ganged up.

Some of you readers might be a little skeptical about what I wrote in the previous sentence. You might think, Tom, nine-year-old boys aren't deeply involved in gang life. The naysayers would be right in one sense, but wrong in another. The fourth-grade punk probably wasn't an active participant in gang life, but his brothers were heavily involved. That gave him a lot of power.

The smaller boy bullied everybody, but singled out big, corn-fed white boys to be his special targets. Over the years, I watched him punch boys to the ground, then recite the litany of who would beat them up. It was just like living with Frank—but at school.

As luck would have it, the smaller boy's street was on the closest route to the local grocery store. I was made aware of that fact the first time I rode my bike to buy a loaf of bread. The smaller boy and a bunch of his compatriots rushed out of a house. They surrounded my bike. One brave soul snuck behind me, put me in a choke hold, and dragged me to the ground. He kept his forearm firmly against my neck. I could barely breathe. I was almost unconscious. My heart was racing.

The smaller boy stepped into my field of vision and said, "Hey, fucking gringo, you ever come down my street again, I will kill you." He flicked open a switchblade to emphasize his point. He bent over and languorously waved the blade in front of my eyes, then made a quick swiping motion in front of my neck.

The smaller boy spit in my face and laughed. The other boys laughed too. The guy who had me in a headlock released me. My head hit the pavement. Hard. Someone kicked me in the ribs and said, "*Pinche gringo puto* (fucking gringo queer)." The group turned and walked back into the house. They laughed and slapped each other on the back. They were celebrating their bravery.

I instantly saw the benefit of taking a longer but safer route to the grocery store. I also pulled a tried-and-true trick from my bag of survival skills; I retreated to the relative safety of my home. That place hosted the best parts of my life. I spent hours with my books, cats, dogs, plants, erector set, record player, and musical instruments.

By the time my eleventh birthday rolled around, I had become a top yard slave. No, our garden wasn't a botanical paradise. But the front lawn was short, green, edged, and weed-free. I had come to an understanding with the weeds in the backyard. I had special plants growing here and there. A flower and vegetable garden. Frank seldom needed to work outside. I thought that was it for the yard-care deal. I didn't realize our small yard was just a starting point for me.

Our development was one of many that grew like cancers in the Santa Clara Valley. Aside from marginal front lawns, the builders

I grew this sunflower when I was twelve. This plant was added to the list of useful things I knew how to grow.

◇◇◇

This photo of Frank is quite rare, because it shows him working in his own backyard. Frank strongly resented doing any sort of manual labor after he got off work. Frank is smiling in this photo, but you can believe he became grumpy after he got drunk and remembered that he had done "Tommy's fuckin' job all day" instead of sitting in a bar. Circa 1965.

sold the properties with bare-dirt yards. Those yards contained the most fertile topsoil on earth. Taken in aggregate, it was lots of lawns, lots of bare backyards, and lots of weeds.

It took hardworking dads and even more children to keep those yards from becoming wildland places. That wasn't a big deal, in those innocent times. Children were less shy about doing manual labor then. The baby boomers were raised by Depression-era parents. Those folks had it rough when they were growing up. Few parents allowed their children to become slackers. They generally trained their children to work, study, and be in good physical condition. The sight of children mowing their parents' lawns was a common one, in any neighborhood.

Many boys took that activity to another level. They used their parents' mower to cut weeds and lawns for other people, for cash. It occurred to me I might be able to do the same thing. This welcome revelation blunted the sting of having to take care of a suburban yard by myself. I could profit from my hard work and experience.

Frank McMillan had tied me to his lawn mower, rake, and hoe. He had unwittingly provided me with valuable tools I could use to earn some pocket money. I cast my net into this new sea of economic activity. So it was that I began my long and illustrious career as a mower of lawns and destroyer of weeds.

5

A WITCH'S COTTAGE IN HELL'S MOST DISTANT SUBURB

I soon discovered that my business plan contained a serious flaw: our neighborhood was overstocked with earnest young boys who had access to their fathers' mowers and a desire to buy comic books. Competition for landscaping jobs was fierce.

I ranged the length and breadth of our huge neighborhood, looking for likely customers. I frequently encountered other mower-pushing boys. We eyed each other like tomcats on a fence as we passed on the sidewalk. But for the most part, it was wasted effort. Jobs were few. People were sick of earnest little boys who knocked on their doors at inopportune times.

My pint-sized commercial yard-work aspirations were saved by architectural considerations. The houses in our neighborhood were hastily built little boxes. They all looked the same. Mile after mile of those ugly homes spread away from the north and east sides of Frank's house. That dynamic shifted on the south side of Senter Road. A long steep-sided hill rose from the road shoulder in that place. When Frank bought his house, the hill was almost bare. A few older, Spanish-style homes dotted the crest. Otherwise, it was covered in wild grasses and flowers.

Farther down Senter Road, an ancient-looking Spanish cottage was tucked onto the end of the hill. It was a relic from the past. Much of the property lazed in the shade of massive blue gum eucalyptus trees. They were primordial forest monsters that had been transplanted into the modern world. A gigantic Chilean pepper tree perfected the gloom of the place.

Most of the dirt that wasn't shaded on the property was covered with desert plants. Huge agaves dotted the west side of the yard. Cactus of every description grew in between. A tiny lawn withered in front of the house. Shrubby tamarisk trees offered a little privacy from road traffic.

The property was bordered on one side by a dusty gravel road, which ran up the spine of the hill. It passed between two tile-roofed watchtowers. The watchtowers obviously belonged to the ancient Spanish cottage. Their shared architecture and building materials betrayed that secret to any who took the time to notice.

Neighborhood kids said, "An old witch lives in the Spanish cottage. Stay away from her. That lady is crazy." The neighborhood kids were scared shitless of the old lady in the Spanish cottage. No one asked if they could mow her lawn. For that reason, I had never asked either.

Things might have gone on like that forever, if I had not been drawn to the abandoned cherry orchard that stood across Senter Road from the Spanish cottage. The trees were gnarled and beautiful in ways that are unique to old members of their kind. A well-thrown stick sometimes released one of the shriveled cherries that remained in the treetops, but that was a rare accomplishment. Competition for those prizes was keen among birds and hungry little boys.

◇◇◇

When Frank bought his house, the steep-sided hill across the road was almost bare. Photo taken from the front yard of our Senter Road home in early summer 1962. The mother and daughter are accepting one of our cat's eight-week-old kittens. The mansion in the photo is on the highest point of Mesa Dolores. Is that structure based on a famous architect's last concepts?

When I played in the cherry orchard, my eye was inevitably drawn to the Spanish cottage on the other side of the road. The tangled plant life always intrigued me. I knew there were interesting species in that place. It occurred to me the old lady who lived there might need a little help caring for her jungle.

I eventually got up my courage and crossed the road. When I walked down the path that led to the front door, I was transported into another world. Behind me was a busy road, derelict orchards, and miles of soulless housing developments. The property in front of me looked as if it had seen no progress since the 1700s. It reminded me of a Spanish version of the ramshackle farmhouses I loved in Texas. But this place was different. It was pure pre-Anglo California. It was magnificent.

Once I walked to the front door, I beheld an ancient iron bell with a rawhide pull hanging from its clapper. Its purpose in that place was obvious. It was the device by which visitors to the property announced themselves. I rang the bell. It sang a pure note that called through the herbal smell of the eucalyptus trees.

I stood there for the longest time, but no one answered the door. That was all right with me. I just wanted to stand and stare at the living museum that surrounded me. I wanted to keep filling my lungs with the clean smell of the trees. I was lost in my reverie. So it was that I was surprised to hear the door open behind me.

When I turned, I found a tiny woman standing behind the barely open door. She had on wire-framed glasses. To me, she looked like a sadder and older version of Mrs. Claus, the wife of the Christmas figure. She asked, "What do you want?"

"Would you like for me to mow your lawn?" I stammered out a response.

I followed her gaze as it wandered toward the lawn. It was about the size of a postage stamp. It was half-dead, not green or vigorous. It plainly did not need to be mowed.

When I saw that she was grasping for a polite way to say, "No," I gave the woman a low-ball price, essentially a free job. That gave her pause. I could tell she was thinking about my offer. I didn't give her a chance to think too long. I said, "I'll clean up the debris that fell from the eucalyptus trees."

That incentive rocked the woman out of her indecision. "Yes, please. They are such messy trees. Ring the bell when you are done." The woman smiled at me and closed the door.

I stood on the front porch for a few moments and collected my thoughts. I was astounded that the woman accepted my offer. I had an "in" to the Spanish paradise! I raced home to get Frank's lawn mower.

When I returned to the Spanish cottage, I did an extra-good garden cleanup. I created a pile of eucalyptus bark, branches, leaves, and seed pods that was taller than I. When I was done, I stood back, exhausted, and admired my work for a few moments. But I didn't rest on my laurels for very long. I knew the difficult part of the job came next—getting paid. People sometimes paid less than they said they would. People sometimes didn't pay anything but harsh words, "Get the hell out of here before I set the dogs on you."

I walked up to the door and rang the bell. The woman answered the door. She was smiling. That was a welcome sight. The woman said, "I have been watching you through the window. You work like a soldier. Would you like to come inside for a glass of water?"

That question gave me pause. I was amazed that she was happy yet afraid to go inside. Frank and Lita told me not to enter strangers' houses. But this woman seemed different. The spirit that dwells within me whispered into my ear, "She's all right, Tommy."

The woman opened the door and stepped aside to let me pass. She pointed toward a small alcove that was filled with an ancient iron table and matching benches. I sat in the appointed place. The woman closed the door. She laboriously shuffled past me. I noticed she was disabled. Each step was accompanied by a grunt or groan of disapproval. She was obviously in great pain.

It took the woman a long time to shuffle into the kitchen and return with a glass of water. The glass tumbler was chipped and scratched.

The woman shuffled sideways and positioned herself in front of the opposite bench. She placed her hands flat on the table top and attempted to lower herself to the bench. She went down a little, yelped with pain, and stood up. She gasped and cursed. The woman repeated this sequence several times before she abandoned any impression of delicacy. She allowed her bottom to unceremoniously plop down on the bench. That strong movement elicited a final yelp from the poor woman.

I quietly watched the sad process unfold. I now realized why it took the woman so long to answer the door when I rang the bell the first time.

The woman sat for a moment and recovered from her exertions, then said, "You look hot. Please drink your water." I did this with great relish. My head was spinning. There was a lot of debris in the yard. It was hot outside. But now I was cool. The temperature inside the cottage was perfect.

I was taught that it wasn't polite to stare, but I couldn't keep my eyes from darting around the room as I drank the water. The inside of the house was a museum. I was surrounded by eighteenth-century artifacts. I didn't know where to look next. The table in front of me was ancient. The iron benches were obviously blacksmith-made. The wall on my left was fronted by a large set of built-in shelves. These were lined with a huge collection of ancient pottery. Artifacts were scattered around the room. There was nothing in my immediate field of vision to indicate that any improvement had been made to the cottage since the last Don sailed back to Spain. I was transfixed.

But the gnome-like woman across from me appeared to be the oldest thing in the room. She seemed so distantly ancient, I almost wondered if she and I spoke the same language. For that reason, if not good manners, I sat like a stone and didn't say a word. The woman obviously had more experience in these matters, because she stuck her hand across the table and said, "I'm Faye. Faye Wolfe." Her formerly pain-ridden face broke into a smile. She looked like an angel to me. Any reservations I had about entering the house melted in the warmth of her gaze.

I shook Faye's hand and said, "I'm Tom Liggett. But most people call me Tommy."

Faye got a serious expression on her face and said, "I have been sitting here, watching you. You work very hard, for one so young."

I shrugged my shoulders and said, "I was raised by hard-working people."

"You have an easy way in the garden. You know what you are doing."

"I have spent my whole life outside. I love plants. I spend every possible moment with them."

Faye clapped her hands together and said, "Really? I love plants too! Isn't this just grand?"

That last word gave me pause. The only time that I heard anyone use *grand* was in a very old movie, to describe a piano, or to refer to a canyon in Arizona. Faye's archaic usage was music to my ears. I thought, here is a ghost from the past. I was entranced.

Faye led the conversation that afternoon. She told me all about her cactus collection. She said, "Some of them are quite rare."

I exclaimed, "Oh, goody! I can clean up your cactus beds too. They are filled with eucalyptus debris."

Faye got a sour look on her face and said, "Oh, my my no! Some of the cacti in those beds have very fine spines. They will break off under your skin. The cholla cactus are especially bad. Their spines blow in the wind. If you don't promise me you won't go into the cactus beds, I won't let you work for me."

That statement got my attention. I didn't want to lose my new job on the first day. There was nothing subtle about Faye's message. It was obvious she didn't want me to get hurt.

"I promise. I will never enter the cactus beds." I meant every word.

My vow was sufficient to defuse the problem. Faye nodded her head and resumed the cactus monologue. "People sometimes steal my cactus, especially the rare ones. I will never become accustomed to finding empty holes where my favorite plants used to grow. But it's worse with some of the other plants. Mexican men knock on my door. They ask if they can tap the blue agave plants. They want to make pulque, a traditional alcoholic beverage. I always tell the men no, but that doesn't stop them. They come in the night and do it anyway."

Faye paused a moment and said, "It's gut wrenching to walk in the garden and discover that someone has used a machete to chop a hole in the heart of a glorious agave plant. They always choose the best ones. The plants die from that treatment."

Faye's cactus problems were alien to me. I was amazed when she mentioned them. I didn't know what to say.

The silence stretched on for a moment, then Faye said, "Oh, my. I was just going on. You said that you like plants too. Tell me all about that."

I said, "I was raised in the orchards. I could identify all the fruit and nut trees when I was three. Some people say I was a lot like Mozart, because I knew so much when I was so young. They called me 'Mozart in the garden.'"

That impressed Faye. She clasped her hands to her face and said, "Oh, my! You are not like other people." That response surprised me. Most people just gave me a bored "uh-huh" when I talked about fruit trees.

Seeing that I had a willing participant in my plant games, I pressed on. I told her about my vast trove of ancient, college-level agricultural books. I waxed poetic about my love for Luther Burbank. "He was the greatest plant man of all time."

Faye agreed.

I was happy she knew about Luther Burbank. Most people didn't.

Faye asked, "Do you grow any fruit trees?"

I said, "Oh, yes! I am trying to emulate Luther Burbank's work. I used to dig almond suckers from abandoned orchards where the roots are three feet deep. But that was hard work. Now I go up in the hills and dig up young, wild almond seedlings. They work the best as rootstocks for grafting stone fruit."

Faye was staring at me, but didn't say anything, so I continued, "I'm always on the lookout for peach, plum, and apricot seedlings. I graft them onto my almond rootstocks. I grow them out. I haven't found a good one yet, but maybe someday I will."

Faye laughed and clapped her hands in amazement. "My, but

you are a grand little boy. I have a seedling apricot growing out in my backyard. Would you like to take cuttings from it?"

I immediately said, "Yes."

Faye's mood shifted. I could tell she wanted to get off the hard iron bench. She asked me to come back the following week to mow her lawn. I said yes. I was pushing the lawn mower down the driveway when Faye shouted, "And bring your pruning shears. You can take cuttings from my apricot seedling."

I waved my arm to acknowledge the suggestion.

I don't remember how much money Faye paid me that day. It wasn't much, but that didn't matter. The music in her voice as she said goodbye was far more valuable to me. I knew I had made a friend. A real friend.

I had a lot to think about as I pushed the lawn mower home. I knew that Faye Wolfe loved plants. I hoped she would teach me more about them. I knew that I had found a replacement for the older friend I left behind at our last apartment. He had taught me a lot about plants and gardening. No matter, I knew something special had happened with Faye.

6

WEAKER THAN MOST BOYS/
STRONGER THAN MOST MEN

Even the best of new friendships can only be carried so far on good intentions alone. That concept was aptly demonstrated when I returned a week later to mow Faye's lawn. As soon as she opened the front door, I chirped, "Well here I am. The mower's all gassed up and ready to go."

Faye got a grave expression on her face and said, "Please come inside."

I nodded my head and walked behind Faye. She motioned toward the iron bench and asked me to sit down. When we were both settled, she began to speak. "I have not been entirely truthful with you. I already have a man who mows my lawn and cleans my yard. His name is Eli. He has worked for me since he was a little boy—almost forty years."

My fantasy world crashed down around my ears. All my hopes and dreams evaporated. I wanted Faye to teach me about plants. I wanted to make money. Frank and Lita hadn't been feeding me well, lately. I was hungry.

Faye read the disappointment on my face. She knew that very few eleven-year-old boys had ambition or reason to persistently seek paying jobs. She knew I needed the money.

Faye quickly filled the silence with a thought. She said, "You made a better job of mowing and cleaning than Eli ever does. He is always in such a hurry. He runs over rare plants with his mower. He chops other plants without being asked."

I thought, so why are you keeping this guy around?

Faye seemed to read my mind. "Eli has a young family to feed."

I thought, oh boy, Tommy. There's the real deal-breaker. You can't take food away from some guy's children.

Faye opened her mouth to say something else but stopped. She was distracted by the battered pickup truck pulling into the driveway. Faye said, "Uh oh. Here comes Eli. We'd better go out and introduce you."

She slowly walked outside. I followed behind. She introduced me to Eli, but he refused to shake my hand. His eyes passed from me to my mower and back to me again. He shot me a hateful glare. I knew his expression well. I have seen crazy Indian stares my whole life. I knew it was an excellent time for me to cede the day—and the job—to Eli.

I tried to say something to Eli, but he turned away from me and began to shout at Faye. I couldn't understand much that Eli was saying to her. He was speaking in an incomprehensible dialect that was comprised of grunts, shouts, and flailing arms.

I quickly ascertained that Eli was deaf. He couldn't hear what he was saying to Faye. She couldn't make Eli understand that I wasn't going to mow the lawn. The more she explained, the angrier he became.

I could smell the rotten alcohol on Eli's breath. No one had to paint a picture of what was happening; I had pissed off a drunken Indian. Life in my family had taught me drunks were a dangerous and unpredictable bunch. I knew that drunken Indians were even worse. My inner voice said, whoa, Tommy, time to back off here.

Eli glared at me some more, then turned and started his mower. He shoved it madly across the lawn. He hit rocks and plants at the end of each pass. Plant bits blew out of the mower's discharge chute. Bits of broken stone and chipped wood whizzed through the air.

I was stunned by the spectacle. I didn't have the sense to duck. Bits of stone and cactus were zipping past my ears.

Poor Faye hobbled toward Eli. He stopped his mad back-and-forth machinations long enough to scream at Faye. She shouted up at Eli's ear. Faye looked like a forest gnome who was trying to reason with an angry elf. Eli ignored her and mowed on. He veered the mower close to Faye's feet as he roared by on the next pass.

Faye's shoulders slumped. She had given up. Faye painfully hobbled back toward the front door. I could tell from her lack of progress that this was the longest journey she had taken in a very long time. Faye paused when she drew abreast of me. She wordlessly gestured toward the house. I fell in behind her. We made quite a pair. She was hobbled by pain. I felt sad and defeated. I knew another great opportunity had been destroyed by someone else's twisted intentions. I trudged along like an old man, as slowly as Faye.

We eventually got back inside the cottage. Faye directed me to sit at the table. She passed by and went into the kitchen. I could hear her rattling through the cupboards. When Faye returned, she had a large tumbler in each hand. One was filled with water.

She set it in front of me. The other contained whiskey and soda water. I recognized the drink. It was Frank's favorite highball. I also noted that Faye's glass was a lot larger than the ones Frank used. It was full to the brim with liquor. No ice. I thought, she's strengthening her resolve with strong drink.

Faye used her last bit of strength to lower herself onto the bench. It took a long time. She groaned a little after she finally plopped down. Faye stared into her glass. She wouldn't look me in the eye. She downed a large portion of the whiskey. Faye eventually looked up from her drink and into my eyes.

"I'm sorry. I was not truthful with you that first day. But something came over me when I saw you standing on my doorstep. You looked like an angel. You were so polite and kind." Faye paused for a moment. "Thin. Far too thin for a boy your age. I just couldn't say no."

Faye's words stunned me. No one had ever said something that nice to me. No one ever seemed to notice there wasn't much fat on my wiry little body. But I was confused. I wasn't at this woman's house to hear nice words. I was hungry. I sat like a stone.

Before I could recover, Faye said, "We'll find something else for you to do around here. Do you know how to do other jobs?"

Oh boy, that was the opening I was looking for. I excitedly said, "I'm good at cleaning bathrooms and doing housework!"

That's not what Faye wanted to hear. She shook her head emphatically and said, "Oh no, you couldn't do that. I have Eva. She is a young Mexican woman. She has a family to feed too."

That sentence threw me for a loop. It was apparent the local indigenous labor force had things locked up tight in that place. I was confused. I thought, if this old lady won't let me work, what does she want from me? Is she truly as crazy as the other kids say?

Faye watched my face as I pondered this rapid change of circumstances. Her expression revealed an important detail; she expected me to bolt out of my seat at any moment. She broke the ice. "You can split firewood for me. The work is not difficult."

Faye's words surprised me, yet again. Her belief that splitting stove wood was "not very difficult" ran counter to anything I had experienced. I had watched men use axes, saws, wedges, and hammers to cut wood since I was a baby. I started helping them, not long after. Wood cutting was not easy work. My head was spinning. I found it impossible to look up from my water glass.

Faye said, "Eli is a carpenter. He brings lumber scraps for me to burn in my stove. The pieces need to be cut, split, carried, and stacked. You can do that."

I instantly accepted the job. I didn't even ask how much I would be paid. I was hungry. Very hungry. I hadn't eaten a decent meal in days. I just wanted to work, get paid, ride across town, and buy a cheeseburger.

Faye was relieved. She led me through the kitchen and into another room. An outside door filled one wall. A small wood-burning stove stood to the right. It had two round lids that could be removed to add small pieces of wood.

I said, "Oh, I have seen a lot of those. They are neat."

Faye shook her head to indicate I was wrong. "This stove is probably a little different from the ones you have seen. It contains pipes that supply hot water to a separate tank. It supplies hot water to the faucets inside of the house."

My eleven-year-old brain saw visions of steam locomotives; I was going to be the brave engineer who fed the firebox. I interjected, "Wow, cool!"

Faye enjoyed my enthusiasm, but she was forced to view the

stove without the romance of my childish locomotive fantasy. The little stove did yeoman duty for Faye. It supplied the only usable heat and hot water in the cottage. She had to fire it when she bathed, washed clothes, or wanted the inside temperature to be much above freezing.

The anteroom was totally devoted to the stove. Its only other furnishing was a large, built-in wood storage box. The wood box was empty. The stove was cold. These facts explained Faye's pressing need to keep me around. She needed a grunt to do the worst job in the place.

Faye said, "Cut and split the wood into small enough pieces to fit through the stove's lids. Split some of it into little bitty pieces. I need that for kindling."

I knew how to make kindling. It was one of the jobs I was expected to do when Frank started fires or barbecues. I was ready for the cutting part too. Frank taught me how to use three types of handsaws when I was four. When I was five, he gave me a pint-sized carpenter's box that included a set of crosscut and rip saws.

Faye opened the outside door. She pointed to a pathway that led along the rear of the cottage and said, "Walk down that way. Go all the way around the house. The woodshed is there."

I walked through the door and started down the path. Faye shouted out, "Stay away from the cholla cactus. If I see you around them, I will send you home."

I nodded my head and waved my right hand to acknowledge Faye's warning. I needed this job. I would not ruin it because of a little boyish exploring.

The pathway made a sharp bend to the left. Just as I was ready to make the turn, Faye called out to me again, "And stay away from Eli. He's unpredictable when he gets this way."

Ah, Faye, my girl. That was an unnecessary admonition. I had only just met Eli, but that was enough for me to determine what I knew about the man: he was a crazy, angry, drunken Indian, and I was the symbol of every bad thing the world had done to him. At that moment, my main purpose in life was to avoid that asshole.

But I didn't ponder drunken Indians or plant thorns for very long. Why? My feet were leading me through the entrance to a dream. Huge cactus surrounded the pathways, which branched and wound away from Faye's side door. These continued out of sight on the steep hillside that rose to the south and east. I was transfixed. I remember thinking there is much to explore here—later. I didn't want to get sidetracked. I needed to find the woodshed.

I walked behind the house and into the glooming shade of a nineteenth-century forest wonderland. Huge eucalyptus trees soared far above my head. I craned my neck backward but couldn't find their tops. These were the monsters I knew from the street view. They were more imposing from this side. I knew their fallen leaves had not seen a rake for many years. The duff under my feet was quite thick. It felt like sponge rubber.

The sight of the trees and garden made a great impression on me. But what I remember best from that first walk on that long-lost day is the smell. It was deep, varied, and powerful. It was redolent of dust, old medicine, and shattered Spanish dreams.

The path eventually fed into a large open area. This place was shaded by a different giant, a Chilean pepper tree. I nodded my head and thought, ah, here is the source of the other smell, stronger than the eucalyptus.

I looked back toward the front of the property and saw the woodshed. It was hung in lean-to style on the side of the cottage. I knew from reading adventure tales that Germanic tribesmen made sheds of like design two thousand years ago. Faye's wood-shed displayed little innovation from that ancient time.

As promised, a small mountain of scrap two-by-fours was piled in front of the woodshed. A medium-sized hatchet was buried in an ancient chopping block. An old crosscut handsaw was hanging from a rusty spike on the wall.

I began to cut and split the wood scraps. Just as Faye had promised, it was easy work. Carrying it the long way to the wood box made my back hurt though. Back then, my back always seemed to be sore. I thought that everyone's back was just like mine. I ignored the pain and pressed on.

In a couple of hours, the wood box was full. I stacked every piece square and neat, piled as high as they would go without spilling. Frank had taught me how to stack wood years before. I called out to Faye, "I'm done."

Faye's answer rang through the air. "Come sit with me in the dining nook."

I stumbled through the kitchen and plopped down on the bench. Now it was my turn to groan a little.

Faye said, "You look hot and tired."

I nodded my head and said, "Yes, but that's okay. I'm used to working. I'll be fine in a little while."

Faye said, "I can tell. But you'll feel better if you wash your face and hands. Go through the stove room and bear to the left. You'll see the bathroom. Be extra careful. The sink is solid porcelain. It will shatter like glass if it is struck by a hard object."

I nodded my head and went to find the bathroom. That small journey took me through Faye's bedroom. The boudoir was a museum. The bed was covered with an old-fashioned feather mattress. The quilt ancient. A small tabletop television provided the only indication that I had not time-traveled back to the eighteenth century.

I noted the sink when I stepped into Faye's bathroom. That finely wrought pedestal was the most beautiful instrument of its type I had ever seen. I washed my face and hands, then dried on a threadbare towel. I trudged back to the dining room and stood in the aisle next to the iron bench.

Faye was enjoying a tall whiskey and soda. She asked me to sit down and have a cool glass of water.

That was not what I wanted to hear. Faye's wood box was larger than it appeared. The promised "easy job" turned out to be a yeoman's task. I was tired and sore. I just wanted to get paid and ride across town for that cheeseburger. But I went along with Faye's idea anyway. I sat down and drained the glass of water in one go.

Faye said, "I am quite pleased with the way you filled the wood box. You work harder than most men I have seen."

My voice said, "Thank you," to Faye, but I didn't quite believe the compliment. I believed I was lazy. Frank, Lita, and my grandmother regularly advised me of that fact.

Faye slid a pile of change across the table. She paid me well and without complaint. I was happy to receive that small mercy. I was too tired to cajole a cheap customer.

Faye told me to get another glass of water and relax for a while. It was obvious that she wanted some company. I didn't want to visit. But I was raised to be polite, so I fetched another glass of water, sat down, and had a sip. I tried to make my growling stomach forget about the cheeseburger that was waiting for me. Diligent practice made me adept at accomplishing that trick.

I silently waited for Faye to begin the conversation. I expected her to talk about plants. That seemed to be our only commonality, as far as I could tell. But Faye didn't speak about botanical matters. She asked about me and my life. That surprised me. No one had ever done that. I always seemed to be in someone's way. I always seemed to speak about topics people found to be boring, like fruit trees, great books, or classical music.

I didn't want to disappoint Faye. So I told her a little about my life. Not my real life, the fantasy version. I delivered the well-rehearsed sacrificial Lita/valiant stepfather Frank speech that had been shoved down my throat since I was born.

Faye smiled, "You are fortunate to have such a loving and wonderful family."

I agreed, as always. I honestly believed I had the best parents in the world. I was done with my story in thirty seconds flat. I squirmed around on the bench. I was bored. I wanted to get the hell out of this strange woman's dining room and go buy a burger. But that's not the way it worked out. Faye rescued the visit. She steered our conversation. By this time, Faye had several ounces of whiskey in her belly. It lowered her inhibitions. Without preamble, Faye got into the story of her life. Turns out it was a real doozy.

7

PARADISE LOST IN A
GREEN VELVET BOX

I have included all the details I eventually gleaned about Faye's life in this book. Of course, she did not reveal all of them at once. The tale was much too big for one telling. The specifics of Faye's life were not appropriate for the ears of an eleven-year-old boy. I had to age a little before Faye went deep. The details and gaps in her story were filled over the five years I knew Faye.

I heard some of the spicier tidbits from Lita much later. She became friends with Faye not long after I did. Lita regularly swapped stories with Faye once they met sometime after I began my wood-chopping duties, and our stories (Lita's and mine) are sometimes eerily similar to Faye's rendition. You'll see. Nonetheless, Faye started strong that first evening, and this is a story within a story:

"I was born in Deadwood, South Dakota, in 1881. It was the epicenter of the last gold rush in the lower forty-eight American states. Deadwood was one of the meanest, roughest places on earth. My mother was a middle-aged prostitute who was at the end of her career. I never met my father. I was an unwanted child."

That concept set bells ringing in my head. I had never met another person whose mother begrudged their child's existence.

Faye gave me a conspiratorial wink and said, "You and I have that in common, don't we?" I was flabbergasted that she had been able to tickle that fine detail from the short personal history I had provided. Faye Wolfe seemed to be prescient in her notions about me. "My mother was not happy to be saddled with an unwanted child late in life. To mark that sadness, she gave me a horrible middle name: Mariah."

I said, "But that is a beautiful name."

Faye snorted, "Ha! You think it's beautiful because you don't know what it means."

"Huh?"

"Mariah means sea of bitterness or child of woe. Some people call an annoying wind a Mariah."

"Oh."

Faye nodded her head and continued, "Yes. My mother imbedded a curse into my name. She damned me for being born."

I huddled over my water glass. That last part struck a nerve. I looked down and responded in a barely audible whisper, "My mother says I ruined her life by being born." I had never admitted that to anyone.

Faye nodded. "By the time I was born, my mother's days of entertaining men for money were over. She supported us by cleaning other people's houses and doing laundry. She also catered weddings and other events. My mother had to work very hard to make ends meet. Sometimes there wasn't enough money to pay for food and rent. We moved from place to place a lot."

I thought, bingo! That is something else we share.

Faye said, "Everyone I knew blamed me for being the cause of my mother's problems. I was too young to know any better, so I willingly accepted that blame. I was my mother's scapegoat. Her beating boy."

Wow, that's what Lita does to me.

Faye said, "I tried to make up for the problems I caused for my mother. I willingly became her slave." An ironic chuckle escaped from Faye's mouth. "As soon as I could walk, my mother made me work."

Faye's mother sounds more and more like Lita.

"When there was no work, I went to school. If my mother needed help, I skipped school. I didn't mind doing other folk's laundry, but I hated the catering gigs. I didn't like working hard while those around me were having fun. But my real problem was with potato chips."

I interjected, "Potato chips, what wrong with them? Everybody likes potato chips."

Faye snorted and said, "Yes, they do, don't they? But did you ever make potato chips from scratch, Tommy?"

"No."

Faye smiled and said, "I didn't think so. If you did, you wouldn't like them so much."

"Why?"

"Potato chips weren't commonly sold in stores, back then. They were made fresh, for immediate consumption. It was a lot of work. The potatoes had to be cleaned and peeled. You had to soak 'em in water, so they wouldn't turn brown. They had to be sliced to transparent thinness on a big, special grater. If you ran them through the grater too quickly, the chips would be too small. Guests expected large, perfectly round potato chips. You had to cut them hard and slow. You had to be careful when you used the grater. It was easy to slice your fingers too. Guests didn't want blood on their fancy potato chips."

I shivered when Faye expressed that last thought. I said, "I help my mother make hash brown potatoes, so I know what it is like to cut your fingers on the grater."

Faye laughed. "Yeah, but those big ol' fashion chip graters were worse. They would take the ends of your fingers right off. But the worst part about making potato chips was the cooking. They were deep fried in lard. We used wood stoves. It was almost impossible to regulate the heat on those monsters. It was very tricky. If you used too little wood, the chips wouldn't cook properly. They would get soggy with grease. Patrons wouldn't eat soggy potato chips. If we got in a hurry and added too much wood, the lard started smoking. The potato chips scorched and tasted bitter. Guests didn't like that either. If the lard got too hot, it burst into flames."

She went on. "Sometimes, you splashed oil onto the stove top. That caught fire too. We were always worried about burning down the kitchen. Everything was made of wood—floors, walls, ceiling, everything. That's why most of the kitchens were in separate sheds, out in the backyard."

Faye laughed. "They always burned down, eventually."

I was flabbergasted. I took potato chips for granted. I didn't know they were such dangerous things.

Faye got a disgusted look on her face and added, "Wedding guests never seemed to get enough of those goddamned potato chips. I spent hours making them. They always yelled for more. My mother couldn't yell back at the guests, so she yelled at me."

Faye paused and took a drink. "My mother and me hated each other. We were cruel in every possible way. That's what happens when you live with someone you despise. Did you know that, Tommy, or are you too young to have determined that out yet?"

I was puzzled by that concept, so I shrugged my shoulders.

Faye continued, "I could tell you lots of stories about my mother. Someday, maybe I will. But I'll tell you the best one now. It is quite funny. My mother got a catering job. It was a wedding. Everything was set to happen in the client's home. One of my friends came along to help with the set-up. We were decorating the client's front room. We were hanging decorative bunting. The host didn't supply a ladder. My mother was standing on a sewing machine, so she could attach bunting to the ceiling lamp."

With amusement Faye went on. "The sewing machine slipped out from under her feet. My mother fell to the floor. She was knocked out cold. Respectable women in those days didn't wear underwear. When my mother fell, her dress bunched up around her waist. My friend and I could see her privates. They were old, hairy, and ugly. My friend and I laughed and said we will never look like that."

Faye began to laugh hysterically. I failed to see any humor in the moment. I didn't say anything. Faye laughed for a while, then took a long drink. "I escaped from my mother's clutches as soon as I turned thirteen."

That comment woke me up. "Wow! How did you do that?" And thus began many of the stories Faye shared with me over those glorious years, over that iron table, sitting on the hard iron benches with glasses in our hands. Hers whiskey. Mine water.

I was working a wedding with my mother. I was cooking those damned potato chips, but it wasn't going well. My mother and I were arguing. I wanted to kill her. My mother took a bowl of potato chips into the house. I concentrated on my work, but was turning the air purple with swear words. All of a sudden, a good-looking man stuck his head in the kitchen door, looked around, and said, "I heard a hell of a racket goin' on in here. Are you all right?"

"There's nothing wrong here that a kitchen fire and a lot of distance wouldn't cure."

The man laughed. "Be careful what you ask for. Some people might arrange anything for a pretty girl like you."

"Even a kitchen fire?"

"Yeah, but that would cause more problems than it would solve. Why don't you just leave, with me, now?"

"My mother would kill me."

"It sounds like she's going to kill you anyway. What have you got to lose?"

I placed the potato skimmer on the counter and pushed the deep-fry kettle to the cool side of the stove. I brushed the hair out of my eyes and took a closer look at my would-be rescuer. I thought, yeah, he's cute, but they all are. But he's better dressed than most of the Romeos I meet around here. He's smooth too. Made me laugh. I think he's okay.

So I removed my apron and threw it on the floor, smoothed my hands down my dress to straighten the fabric and looked at the man. "Where are we headed? I don't care as long as it's a long way from Deadwood, South Dakota."

I interrupted, "You didn't really leave Deadwood with the guy, did you? I mean, he was a total stranger."

"Tommy, when you don't have any chances, you grab at the first one that comes along. I hope it never gets so bad you understand what I mean."

That sentence made me feel humble. I was embarrassed. It sounded like I was judging Faye. "I'm sorry. Please go on with your story."

Faye nodded her head and smiled. "Hold on." She slowly raised herself from the bench and shuffled into a back room. Faye emerged a few minutes later carrying a box. I recognized the type—a flower box, the kind florists use to deliver bouquets of long-stemmed roses. But this box was older than any I had ever seen. It was covered with faded green velvet and tied with a fancy satin ribbon.

Faye placed the box on the table and slowly sat down. She caressed the top of the box with both hands and said, "A wonderful man gave me a dozen American Beauty roses in this box. I will treasure that memory forever." She gently untied the ribbon and opened the flower box. When she raised the lid, I could see it was filled with hundreds of photographs. Faye sorted through the photographs. She was lost in her own world, old memories resuscitated in black and white.

Faye handed me photographs, one at a time. They depicted Faye at parties. A different man sat next to Faye in each photograph, never the same one twice. The photographic backdrops were lovely. They were shot in fancy ballrooms. I saw acres of white linen and sparkling tableware. Liquor bottles and wine glasses were scattered everywhere. Huge drifts of Victorian flower arrangements dominated the background, mountains of them. Beautiful, well-dressed women and handsome men completed the photographic ensembles.

But everything and everyone paled next to Faye. The photographs were all staged around her. I could see why; Faye stood out. She was gorgeous. She looked like Clara Bow, the silent film actress of a later era.

Faye didn't say much about the photographs. She was sorting through them as quickly as possible. I could tell she was looking for a particular photograph. Her expression changed when she found the right one. She handed the photograph to me.

The image depicted a riverine setting. Faye was sitting on the rear bench of a small rowboat. The boat was floating in a cypress swamp. Huge trees filled the surroundings. Faye was wearing a ruffled white evening gown that contained at least ten or twelve yards of fine muslin. She was holding a white frilly parasol in one hand and a cane fishing pole in the other. A handsome, well-dressed man was sitting in the boat next to Faye.

I looked at the photograph for a moment and laughed. "That is a fancy dress to be wearing on a fishing trip."

Faye nodded and smiled. "Turn it over. Read the caption aloud."

"It says, fishing for suckers."

Faye snorted, "He sure did catch a big sucker that day. Me! I thought he was gonna be my boyfriend, husband even. Settle down. Have kids, the whole deal. But it didn't turn out that way. He was just looking out for himself. He was a real shit heel."

Faye got quiet for a moment. She opened her mouth to say something, then looked me in the eye and stopped.

I saw Faye's discomfiture and offered her a lifeline, "It's okay, Faye, just tell me what you want."

Faye nodded her head. "The man in the photograph introduced me to rich men, mostly older. Those guys had boring days and harping wives. They wanted to cut loose at night, listen to music, dance. Eat and drink in the best places. Spend time with young women. They were willing to pay money, big money, to be with the right girl."

My face reddened and I said, "Oh." This was beginning to sound a lot like the ribald tales I read in *Playboy* magazine.

Faye nodded her head. "He said he was my boyfriend, but he was really my pimp." Faye winced when she said that last word. I could tell she hated the sound and what it denoted.

Faye looked down at her glass. She couldn't meet my eye. Faye was quiet for a while. "But he showed me an easier way to make money than washing other people's shitty underwear and making goddamned potato chips."

I instantly hated the anonymous man in the photograph, but I wanted to hear more of the story. "What happened to him?"

Faye got a pained expression on her face. "He left with another girl, in the middle of the night, took all my money and jewelry with him. He stiffed me for the cost of the hotel room and left me holding the bag. The fat, greasy hotel manager gave me three choices: get busted for defrauding an innkeeper, wash dishes for a month to work off the tab, or, well, you know, Tommy."

I looked at Faye but didn't say anything. She nodded her head and sighed. "This is a raw subject for a little kid. Are you sure you want to hear more?"

The story was just getting interesting. I didn't want Faye to stop talking, so I said, "I hear about this kind of stuff all the time at family parties."

Faye nodded her head. "I got smarter after my first boyfriend.

I began to see my body as my business. Kind of like what my mother did, but without the potato chips."

We broke into laughter when she dropped the potato chip line. Faye sure knew how to tell a joke.

"It was all fast times and shady characters. I was living a life I couldn't have, by being a regular stiff. But that's the dirty little secret about working girls, Tommy. Many of them enjoy the life. The money and clothes. Living in fancy places with nice furniture. The attention they get from men—until the money runs out, that is. Anyway, I was living the high life. That's what I call the Faye part of my name. The good part. But come what may, the accursed Mariah part of my name always brought me down."

8

ALL OF MY NAMES
END WITH MARIAH

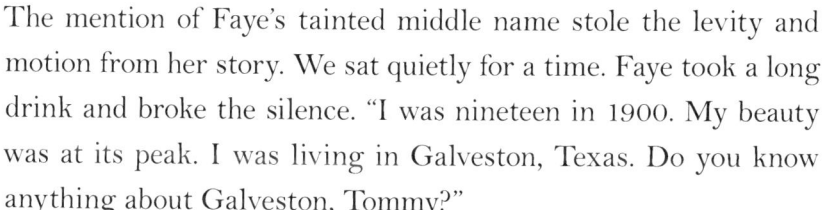

The mention of Faye's tainted middle name stole the levity and motion from her story. We sat quietly for a time. Faye took a long drink and broke the silence. "I was nineteen in 1900. My beauty was at its peak. I was living in Galveston, Texas. Do you know anything about Galveston, Tommy?"

That question perked me up. "We go to the beach there when we visit relatives in Texas. The water is warm as a bathtub, not freezing cold, like in California."

Faye smiled and said, "Ah, yes. The Texas beaches are grand. But I wasn't there for the sand and surf. When I lived in Galveston, it was the largest city in Texas. It had the busiest seaport in America. More cotton was shipped from Galveston than anywhere else in the world. Wages were high for everybody. Lots of people made money, big money, sometimes. It was a boom town, just like Deadwood, but better. Places to eat, gamble, and dance were everywhere. Hordes of people were passing through, so Galveston was always packed with people—and money."

Faye paused for a few moments. I could tell she was thinking about what to say next by choosing her words carefully, so they would suit the ears of a young boy. "Guys who make lots of money liked to spend it—sometimes on girls like me. But what I liked most about Galveston was that it was freewheeling. We didn't get harassed by the cops, unlike some of the other towns I worked. The cops were on the tab, everything went smooth, as long as everybody played fair. The cops didn't want visitors to leave Galveston with a bad impression."

Faye's comments surprised me. "Wow!" I said. "I thought Galveston was just a funky little town."

Faye snorted. "It was called the sin city of the Gulf."

Faye grew quiet and fiddled with her glass before she resumed. "I wish it could have stayed that way forever. But it didn't."

"Why?" I wondered. And then her story took a surprising turn.

They say Galveston is built on an island, but that's not really true. Calling it an island assigns a level of permanence that is not deserved. Galveston is a sandbar, nothing more.

Hurricanes regularly crash ashore from the Gulf of Mexico. When that happens, sandbars are created, changed, and destroyed. Sandbars are like dice. When they get thrown by a storm, they always come out in different configurations. Anyone who has lived around the Gulf of Mexico knows that. Folks in 1900 knew it too. The smart ones were nervous. They remembered the hurricanes that destroyed Indianola, Texas, a few years before. Nearly five hundred people were killed, in a time when there weren't many people around.

Folks in Galveston knew their lives rested on a sandpile that barely rose above sea level. Some people wanted to build a seawall to protect Galveston from hurricanes. But they were in the minority. Most Galveston residents saw no reason to build a barrier. They knew their city had survived many previous storms. They thought it could survive future ones without a seawall. Most Galveston residents believed the city couldn't afford the cost, and it became a contentious issue in local politics. The people who wanted to build a seawall couldn't get enough support.

Isaac Cline was the local director of the Galveston weather bureau. He wrote an official meteorological statement about the risks Galveston faced from storms. Cline published his opinions in the *Galveston Daily News*. He wrote that the seawall was not necessary to protect the city. Cline believed that it was "impossible for a hurricane of significant strength to strike the island."

The seawall didn't get built. Shortsighted people made matters even worse. Wind and water deposited large sand dunes on the seaward shore of Galveston Island. The dunes acted like a natural seawall. They blunted the force of storms that came in from the Gulf of Mexico. Developers scraped up the seaward dunes and hauled them away. They used the sand to fill in low spots around the island, to create more land for development. They unwittingly removed the only natural barrier against Gulf storms.

I was living in a ritzy Galveston hotel during the first week of September in 1900. I had a bunch of rich boyfriends. They took care of all my needs, even some I didn't know I had. I was drinking chilled French champagne every night. I had fine clothes and jewelry— good jewelry, not that fake stuff.

Local newspapers mentioned that a storm was headed toward the American coastline. I had been through lots of Gulf thunderstorms by then. I thought nothing about the one that was coming. I wasn't the only person who had that casual attitude. Most people in Galveston didn't take the storm threat seriously. They believed that the storm wouldn't hit them. Even if it did, they thought the city would be just fine. It was an easy fiction to believe. The weather was clear and nice. The ocean was like bathwater. Who was worried about a silly old storm?

Oh, Tommy, we didn't know the newspapers were not accurate. Official US government sources didn't want to cause panic among those who lived in the paths of hurricanes. So, do you know what they did?

The government called hurricanes storms, and they made them seem less harmful than they were. But our casual attitude went beyond believing the government's scripted fiction. American weather forecasters bungled the forecast. They said the storm was going to sweep up the Eastern Atlantic coast. Cuban weather forecasters strenuously disagreed with that presumption. They believed the storm would veer north, into the Gulf of Mexico and come ashore on the central Texas coast.

The Galveston weather bureau finally hoisted storm warning flags on the afternoon of September 7. Most people didn't take that knowledge very seriously. We thought the storm would come, then go. Very few people left the island.

Boy, were we wrong. On the evening of September eighth, a category four hurricane crashed ashore just west of the city of Galveston. Local wind-measuring instruments indicated the highest recorded wind speed was 120 miles per hour, right before the instruments were destroyed.

Most of the buildings in Galveston were hastily built wooden boxes. A third of them were blown apart by the raging wind. It got worse from there. The highest point on Galveston was only about eight feet above sea level. The storm surge was over fifteen feet. It washed over the entire island. Buildings got knocked off their foundations by the surging water. They were swept along and smashed to pieces by the island-covering surf.

It was horrible. One minute, I was standing with a glass of whiskey in my hand, watching the walls shake and rattle. The next minute, the wall in front of me collapsed. It peeled away from the ceiling like the top card off a deck. The floor collapsed. I was thrown into the water. Hell, what am I saying? It wasn't like pool water. It felt like I was in the middle of an eggbeater.

But the wind—oh lord, Tommy, the wind was screaming. It was like it was alive. It sounded like a bomb was going off. Stuff was blowing in the wind. Roof shingles, sections of walls. A lady's hat. It didn't occur to me to swim. I couldn't have done so if I had tried. I never learned. I was just swept on top, along with the other crap in the water. I finally managed to latch onto a big timber. I held onto that sucker for dear life.

The water was deep—up to the second-story windows of the remaining structures. I tried to grab a porch railing as I swept by, but the building crumpled as I approached. The pieces swept ahead of me.

Me and that timber just banged and bounced through the water. The wind kept trying to pull me off. I hugged it tighter. I was knocked against a house that seemed to be a little stronger than the others. I managed to grab a drain pipe that was sticking out from the wall. It took all I could do just to hold on.

I watched a bunch of people float along in the water. Most of them weren't as lucky as me—they weren't moving. One man went right past me. He was half-dead, but moving. I reached out to grab his arm, but I damn near lost my grip on the drain pipe. I let that man go on by. I wish I could have saved him.

I held on to that pipe for hours. My arms were cramped with the effort. But the storm eventually passed. The water level dropped. I saw a little porch on the side of the building. I crawled up and collapsed. I was exhausted. I fell asleep.

A few hours later, I woke up. I was lying in the mud that had accumulated on the porch. I was dazed and groggy.

When I could gather my wits a little, I raised up on my elbows and looked down at myself. I was dressed in a corset and a ripped dressing gown. I had one torn stocking, no shoes. I looked down at my bare feet. My toes were shriveled like prunes from the water and mud.

It's funny how you remember an insignificant little detail like that, isn't it, Tommy?

I had no idea what Faye was talking about, but I nodded my head to affirm the notion. I didn't know what to say.

Faye got a sad look on her face, then stuck her foot out at me. She shook the slipper off her foot and said, "Look at my poor little foot now. The toes are all twisted. The nails are like dog claws. No man would pay to look at those toes now, would he, Tommy?"

That statement shocked me. I began to feel uncomfortable. I squirmed around on the bench. I was just a kid, but people had been trying to get seriously sexy with me since I was five. I knew damn well where that shit usually ended: Someone tried to get me to touch their private parts or allow them to touch mine. I damn sure knew I didn't want to touch any parts of the eighty-one-year-old semi-stranger who was dangling her horrid-looking foot in front of me. I stared down at the tabletop.

But for once my worst fears didn't play out that way. Faye replaced her foot in the slipper and pulled her leg back under the table.

Faye took a long, slow pull from her glass and continued the story.

I was dazed and cold. I felt like I was sitting in a swampy junkyard. Piles of debris were everywhere. Just a few buildings were standing. Those that were in one piece were knocked off their foundations and leaned at crazy angles.

The main flood was gone, but water was everywhere. Puddles. Pools. New stream beds replaced streets and sidewalks. And mud. Oh, Lord, that damn mud. Mucky, stinky sand. It was drifted and piled everywhere.

I didn't see many people. The ones I saw were staggering around like they were drunk. They looked dazed, ragged, and washed-out, like ghosts. I sat there in the mud for the longest time. I didn't know what to do.

If it was left up to me, I would probably still be sitting there in the mud. But a man I knew came along. He wasn't much better off than me, but at least he was standing. The man ran over to where I was sitting and said, "Faye, Faye? Is that you?"

"Yeah, it's me."

We talked for just a moment, then the man grabbed my arm and pulled me up. I couldn't stand on my own. My legs were wobbly. He had to hold on to me.

The man asked me if I was all right. I never thought to notice, before he asked. When I took stock of my various parts, I noted cuts, scrapes, and bruises all over my body—even on my titty. It was sticking out of my torn dressing gown.

I became really embarrassed when I heard Faye use the word titty. Not because of the reference to female parts. I was used to that. Lita ran naked around the house whenever my stepfather wasn't around. I just didn't expect to hear the word titty pop out of nowhere. That was not a word I was accustomed to hear in polite conversation. Like from someone who paid you to split wood.

Faye noticed my embarrassment and got a sad expression on her face. "I'm sorry I used that word, Tommy. I just got carried away with my story."

"That's okay. The women in my family talk about everything around me."

"Good. That's the way it should be. If there were more like your mother, men wouldn't be so mystified by women."

That last sentence confused me. I didn't get the philosophical gist of what Faye was saying. I was still thinking about her story. I'd heard a lot of stories, but never one like this.

Faye stared into her glass for the longest time. She eventually looked up at me. "I forgot that I was talking with a child. You are such an old soul, Tommy."

It took me years to realize that Faye had discerned another facet of my upbringing; I was raised by people who hated children. My daily survival was predicated by one concept: I had to act like I was an adult, even when I didn't know what I was supposed to do.

The silence stretched on. Faye eventually asked, "Have you heard enough of an old woman's ramblings for one day, Tommy?"

That question woke me up. I was enjoying Faye's story. I wanted to hear how it ended. "Oh, no! Please tell me how you got out of the mud—in Galveston."

My response tickled Faye. She laughed until she cried. "You are an angel. God sent you to remind me there is still love in the world." Faye clapped her hands together and said, "Oh my! I have just thought of a perfect name for you. I will call you Lovey."

I felt a red flush creeping across my face. My ears were burning. No one had ever said such nice things to me. I didn't know how to handle it, so I looked down at my lap.

Faye looked embarrassed too. "Oh, I'm sorry. I barely know you and here I am, saying these silly things."

Neither one of us said anything for a few moments. It was my turn to break the silence. I almost whispered when I said, "I like you, too, Faye. But could you please tell me the rest of the story?"

My words erased Faye's sad look. She began to smile. Faye understood that she had a good audience. She really got into her story.

The guy took off his suit coat and draped it over my shoulders. He was a big man. The coat hung down to the middle of my thighs. We heard voices coming from inside the house. We pushed through the mud and sand that was blocking a side door and went in. We walked upstairs. The walls and ceiling were intact, but not much else. The windows were blown out. The wind had surged through the rooms. Things were scattered all over the place. Everything was soggy.

We found a bunch of people gathered in an upstairs room. Some of them were huddled on the floor, asleep. Others were milling around, having quiet conversations. The people were cold and wet, but none was as miserable looking as me. But the men were healthy enough to leer at me when I came into the room.

But the women weren't so kind. I could read their faces. They were scandalized by how I was dressed. My rescuer's jacket was cut pretty long, but not long enough to cover what should have been hidden.

One of those snooty old broads was braver than the rest. I guess it was her house. She walked over and told me she had a dress for me. She took me into another room and rummaged through a large storage chest. She pulled out a dress and showed it to me. It was a frilly evening gown that was made of bright, emerald green satin, so shiny it almost made my eyes hurt to look at it. It looked like it was made for a woman who stood about five ten and weighed 250 pounds. I was five even and weighed 110. I knew that damned dress was going to look like a circus tent on me. The woman who gave me the dress was enjoying the moment. She stuck her nose up in the air and told me, it's all I have for you. Take it or leave it.

I looked that old bitch in the eye, snatched the dress out of her hands, and said, "Fine, get me a pair of scissors and leave me alone. I'm a lady. I like to change in private."

Tommy, you should have seen the look on that woman's face. She almost passed out. I don't think anyone ever told her what to do in her own house.

The woman who gave me the dress got the parting shot, though. She handed me the scissors, then told me to fix the gown, get dressed, and get out. And you know, Tommy, she pointed at the side door of the house when she said that, the one servants use. But I knew I was beat. I needed that dress, so I kept my mouth shut.

I used the scissors to cut off about a foot of material from the bottom of the dress. I cut it into strips. I tied that dress in all the right places. I looked down at myself in a piece of broken mirror on the floor. I looked good.

I looked over my shoulder to make sure nobody was watching me and walked over to the snooty lady's storage chest. I opened the lid and poked around inside. I found a pair of riding boots and some socks. They were made for a boy. They fit like they were made for me.

I grabbed a linen bonnet from the bottom of the chest, the kind old ladies wore to church. I pulled it over my head and looked around the room. The place was a mess. Stuff was scattered everywhere. I still needed a certain item. But where would I find it? I found a soggy hatbox. It contained a hideous Easter creation, years out of date. But I wasn't interested in the hat. I wanted the fancy pin that was stuck through the crown.

Ladies used to wear fine hats. Big hats. They needed very long pins to attach the hats to their hair so the hats wouldn't blow off in the wind. Some of those pins were six, eight, even twelve inches long. They were needle-sharp on one end and thick on the other, with a good knob to hold onto.

A pretty girl needs some protection. Sometimes ya just have to make people get the point, when you don't want to get bothered.

I must have looked perplexed about the pin, but I finally understood. I was raised in ghettoes. Faye got herself a shiv. A pokey thing. A weapon. I was floored. I generally associated that type of behavior with Mexican toughs and white hooligans. I was a quick boy. I jumped right in with the main question, "Did you ever use the hatpin on anybody?"

Faye shot me an indignant look and said, "There are certain questions you never ask people, Tommy. That was one of them." Faye glared at me for a moment to emphasize her point.

My question changed the tenor of our visit. Or maybe it was the tumbler full of whiskey, which was coursing through Faye's bloodstream. She said, "Oh, my. Look out the window. It's dark. Isn't this a school night?"

I sighed, "Yes, ma'am, it is."

Faye said, "Then I think you should go home."

I agreed but asked, "Please Faye, tell me, how did you get out of the mud in Galveston?"

Faye struck a model's pose and said, "It was easy. A pretty girl with smarts always lands on her feet." The firm tone Faye used to deliver that line signaled the end of the evening. She began the arduous process of raising herself from the iron bench.

I stood and discovered that I was stiff and sore too.

Faye noticed my condition. "The wood box is larger than it appeared, isn't it?"

I mumbled, "Yes."

Faye said, "I'm certain you have a hot meal and warm bath waiting for you at home. That will make you feel much better."

I nodded my head, "Yes, ma'am." I didn't meet Faye's eyes as I said those words. It was a lie. Lita was working the night shift. Frank was at the bar. Our house was cold and dark. It contained no food. That's why I filled Faye Wolfe's wood box; I needed money to buy dinner. But I was too tired to pedal my bicycle two miles each way to get a burger. I turned, gave Faye a hug, and shuffled toward the front door.

Faye called to me, "Oh no, Tommy, not that way. That door is for company. The side door is for family. Please use that one."

Faye's words brightened my tired mood. I turned and walked back toward the door. She stopped me as I passed, reached up, and hugged me again. "Good night, Lovey. Sweet dreams."

I nodded my head and went out the side door. The family door.

9

THE HUMAN PUNCHING BAG

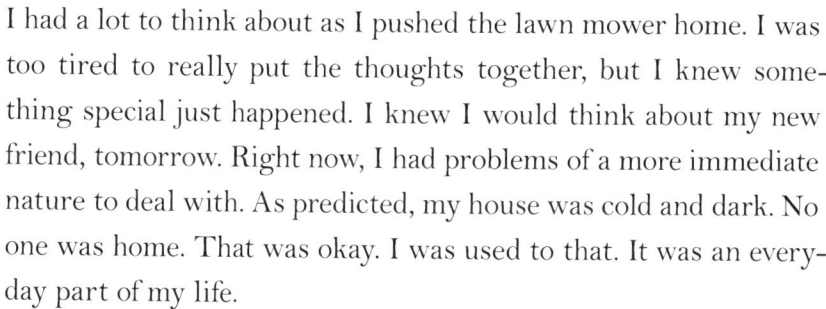

I had a lot to think about as I pushed the lawn mower home. I was too tired to really put the thoughts together, but I knew something special just happened. I knew I would think about my new friend, tomorrow. Right now, I had problems of a more immediate nature to deal with. As predicted, my house was cold and dark. No one was home. That was okay. I was used to that. It was an everyday part of my life.

I knew there was no food in the house, but I had to look anyway. It was a regular goodnight ritual. I began with the refrigerator where I found a crusty jar of French's mustard and three bottles of Lone Star beer—a gift to Frank from someone in Texas.

Next, I moved to the lower kitchen cabinets. I had to get down on my hands and knees to do that. My back hurt too much to bend. The cabinets contained a rotting can of tropical fruit punch and two odiferous, desiccated potatoes. Not even a classical Inca would have eaten those rotten things.

I moved to the middle cabinets. They contained a crystalized jar of Brer Rabbit unsulfured molasses and a can of sardines in ketchup. I always had the same thought when I saw them: I'll fuckin' starve to death before I eat that shit.

At the final station of my food-seeking ritual, I looked in the top cabinets. A chair made a fine ladder to accomplish that purpose. I looked through every high cabinet in the kitchen. I moved every dish and plate looking for hidden morsels. I found dusty pots and pans and a mousetrap (no mouse).

I got down from the chair and dragged it into the dining room. I turned around and looked back into the kitchen. I wanted to make sure that I hadn't missed any food-containing places. I knew the answer to that question before I began my search. I had that empty kitchen memorized.

I sighed and told myself, you're not that hungry anyway. The sloppy joe sandwich you had for lunch was really filling. I knew that line of reasoning by heart. My brain got lots of practice; it made uncounted vain attempts to convince my stomach it had eaten a wholesome meal in the last few hours or days.

I walked into my room and undressed. Sawdust and splinters fell onto the floor. They reminded me of the work I accomplished. They reminded me of Faye's story. I felt sorry for her, sitting alone in a cold house. It didn't occur to me to feel sorry for myself for being in a similar situation. Do you believe that behavior marks me as a saint? Not at all. You see, I knew that I was better off when I was alone. When I was alone, I wasn't belittled, hit, or kicked.

Frank proved the validity of that concept later in the evening. He got home from the bar at midnight. How do I know the time, after fifty-seven years? Because Lita got home at 12:30. There would have been high, holy hell to pay if Lita got home before Frank on a work night.

Frank normally didn't want to leave the bar that early. He believed he was the most handsome, witty, and generous guy at the Rock Castle bar, the life of the party. He believed no one

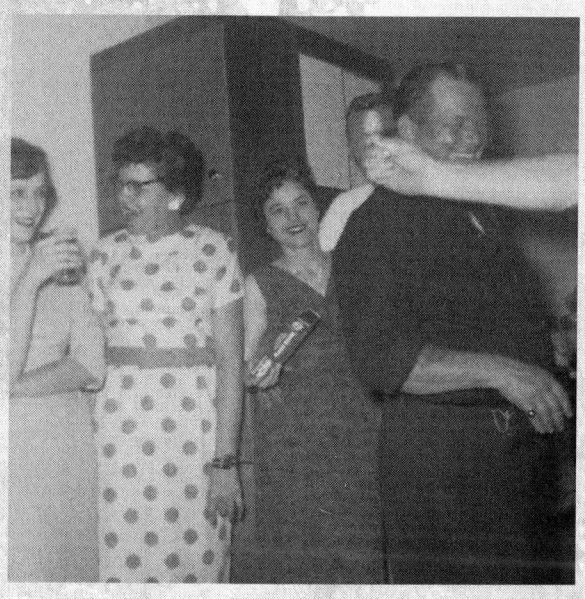

✧✧✧

The kitchen at our new house on Senter Road. I had
these cabinets memorized for their food-containing
possibilities long before this photo was taken at Frank
and Lita's housewarming. As per usual, I stepped in as
the event's reserve photographer, when Lita wanted to
be in the shot. My grandmother Ruby is on Lita's left.
The laughing man on the right is Frank's ex-boss and
longtime drinking buddy, Bob Flaherty. October 1960.

wanted him to go home. Frank wanted to stay until closing at two and buy a round for the house when the bartender made the last call, then go into the owner's shitty upstairs apartment and have another drink to properly finish off the evening.

Other times, Frank couldn't get out of a tavern quickly enough. Frank thought he was a Romeo, but women spurned his amorous advances. Sometimes Frank got into fistfights with other men. Sometimes Frank spent his entire paycheck at the bar.

Any way you cut it, Frank McMillan was not happy when he pushed through the bar's swinging door. He festered and stewed on the long drive home. Frank knew that as soon as he got there, his real problems would be waiting. His nagging wife and ungrateful stepchild lived in that place. Frank knew he would only get a few hours of sleep before he had to do eight hours of hard manual labor. He knew he would nurse a hangover all through the next day.

By the time Frank got home, he was royally pissed off and snarling mad. Frank needed an outlet for his frustrations. He couldn't yell at his asshole boss. The man would have fired him on the spot. Frank needed a high-paying job to fund his endless bacchanal. Frank damned sure couldn't go off on Lita without igniting her thermonuclear temper. She'd scream in his face, pummel him with her fists, and kick him out of the house. The loss of Lita's money and housekeeping skills would destroy the framework Frank needed to support his extracurricular parties.

But the rules were different as they applied to little Tommy Liggett. Frank could do anything he wanted to me. There was no one around to see what he did to me. I became Frank McMillan's human punching bag, his little post–bad bar night stress reliever. That played out in a lot of different ways. It took Frank seven years to accumulate and refine his techniques. He worked

Lita at the peak of her beauty. The photo caption
reads: "Frank; Especially Yours, Love—Lita." Frank
was married to the prettiest girl in town, but he
went trolling for bar flies several times a week.

◇◇◇

I spent a lot of time waiting for Frank inside and outside of
the Rock Castle in San Jose, California. I knew many of its
regular customers on sight and by name. The lady on Frank's
right seemed to always be in the bar, sitting on the same stool.
She always had a cigarette going. Frank said, "At one time
or another, ev'ry man in the place gave her a good poking."

A racy ashtray from a low-rent bar. Lots of roughnecks and loose women hung out at the Rock Castle. Frank McMillan could have bought a bunch of houses with the money he left in that place.

◇◇◇

Lita and Frank in the Rock Castle, 1965. This photo catches the true spirit of the people involved; Lita is showing much more leg than was appropriate for the era. Don't mention what she's doing with her left hand. For his part, Frank is in pig heaven; the prettiest girl anyone ever saw is giving him the 1965 version of a lap dance. Note the look on the man who is standing behind the horny couple; that dude wants to be Frank. When Lita got pissed enough, the other man could have taken Frank's place for a night— or three. Who knows?

◇◇◇

Frank McMillan, drunk and pissed off in his kitchen.
Christmas Eve, 1959. Note Lita's left hand; she is handing
Frank a straight shot of whiskey in a vain attempt to
placate him. I took this photograph and can state with
absolute certainty that Frank was glaring at me. His
look said, "You got too many fuckin' Christmas presents
tonight. I never got no presents when I was a kid. I can't
wait for all these folks to leave so I can tear you up." He
did, repeatedly. Merry fucking Christmas, Tommy.

through countless variations before he settled on a suite of abuses that was the most effective.

Frank played out his favorite abuses at night. I slept on the living room floor at our old apartment. Two blankets, one pillow, and one sheet made my bed. Frank crept into the room. He didn't turn on the light. He did his best work in the dark. Frank pulled away the blanket and grabbed hold of my T-shirt. He snatched me up like a rag doll and smashed my body into the wall. The force of that blow knocked my breath away. I was stunned. Frank silently held me against the wall for a few seconds. He was savoring the moment.

Frank leaned toward me. His whiskery mouth was two inches from my ear. He emitted a nauseating miasma of rotten whiskey. Frank began to scream in my ear. If I live to be 129 years old, I will never forget Frank's words: "What are you doin' a-lyin' up there in the bed? Why ain't you out there a-helpin' me make some money for the house?"

That was a rhetorical question. Frank didn't wait for a response. He went into an all-purpose rant. He yelled about my sloth and generally evil nature. He finished with the simple declaration that all his problems arose because I was living in his house.

Each of Frank's sentences was punctuated the same way: He slammed me into the wall. Every slam knocked the breath from my lungs. I had the same thought each time he repeated that type of nighttime predation: Frank is finally going to kill me.

Wow! Pretty bad, huh? But guess what? That behavior got worse after we moved into our new house. Why? Because Frank and Lita bought me a real bed. That's where I was sleeping when Frank reached under the frame and lifted the bed off the floor. He rotated the bed 90 degrees and slammed it into the wall. My face and body hit the wall hard, driven by all of Frank's strength and the inertia of the rapidly moving bedframe and mattress. Frank released me. I ended up face down on the concrete floor. I was the bottom pancake in a stack that included the mattress, bed linens, broken bed slats, and frame.

Frank pulled the mattress off the pile and sailed it across the room like it was a child's toy. He was stoked. Frank reached into the debris and pulled me up. He began the usual smash-Tommy-against-the wall routine. That sonofabitch even used the same words. But I can assure you that I was not bored by the repetitive nature of Frank's monologue. He had my full attention.

After Frank had enough fun for one night, he threw me into the wreckage on the floor. He glared down at me and said, "Would ya' look at this fuckin' mess? You are a pig! Clean this shit up, right now! I come in here tomorrow, this place better be fuckin' spotless. Do you hear me?"

I said, "Yes, sir. It will be spotless when you get up in the morning, sir." Frank staggered out of the room and slammed the door.

I remained in the wreckage of my bed for a little while. I wanted to determine if Frank would return for another round of wall smashing. Experience taught me I suffered less pain when Frank found me in a prone position. I made an easier target when standing. When I believed he wasn't coming back, I tried to stand up. That didn't work out too well; my back hurt like crazy. My knees buckled from the pain. I tripped on a broken bed slat and fell to the floor. I uttered a cry of pain and remained on the floor.

A few seconds later, the door the flew open and smashed against the wall. Frank charged into the room and bellowed, "What the fuck are you a doin' in here? How the fuck is a man supposed to get some sleep in his own fuckin' house with you a yellin' like that?" Frank didn't wait for an answer. "And why ain't you cleaned up this fuckin' pigsty, yet? Do you think I bought this place for you to slop up like this?"

"No, sir."

Frank tried to glare at me some more, but he couldn't focus his eyes. He was too drunk. He swayed back and forth on his feet for a few seconds. I tensed up. I thought he was going to tear into me, again. But he didn't do that. Frank was just trying to remember how his feet worked. He eventually solved that problem. He turned and left the room.

I crawled away from my bed on hands and knees. I grabbed the door knob and pulled myself up. A shooting pain flashed across my back muscles as I stood. I almost cried out, but bit my lip. I didn't want to learn what would happen if Frank came into my room for an unprecedented third time in a single evening.

I turned and looked around my room. Frank's carefully tossed mattress had smashed against a dresser, spilling its contents on the floor. Clothes were scattered everywhere. I sighed and wished for the good old days at our previous apartment. I didn't have as much to clean after Frank's nighttime ministrations.

It took me a good while to piece together the remains of my bed. I placed the broken slats under the middle of the mattress, where they couldn't be seen. I made the bed the way Frank liked it—military style, with hospital corners. You could have bounced a quarter off the top blanket.

I crawled under the covers and tried to go to sleep. That didn't happen. Sleep generally eluded me on the nights Frank really beat me up. On one level, I was afraid Frank would come back for another round of fun. But the real cause for my sleeplessness was far more sinister.

Frank had been in my life since I was four. He immediately began a program of strangely twisted Bible reading. You see, Frank read aloud from the Bible each night he was home. He would then pick it apart and reveal what he called "the lies." If I tried to go to any church more than one time, he accompanied me. We sat in the back row. Frank whispered in my ear as the preacher made each point in the sermon. Frank revealed the lies in the preacher's words. He was a better orator than any preacher I ever heard.

But none of that mattered to me. I still believed in the Christian god. Let's take that a step further; Frank was just one of many people who regularly told me I was going to hell. Frank, Lita, and my grandmother told me thousands of times that I was a lazy, greedy, evil, ne'er-do-well. The combination of those concepts left no doubt in my mind about possible outcomes; I was beyond redemption. I was going to hell. Not after I died, but now.

I believed that Satan was about to rise through the floor, grasp me with his claws, and drag me down to his storied kingdom. I sometimes got so worked up, I believed that Satan was on his way, that he would be here in a few minutes! I was scared out of my wits. My heart was racing. I thought it would explode. I knew I was doomed, but spent hours in prayer trying to lessen the damage.

My prayers were always of like kind. They never contained any hope that I would receive redemption. It was all cut-and-dried stuff; come what may, I was going to hell. Period. Done deal. I recited those prayers over and over again. Then I began to ask forgiveness for praying in "vain repetition." The murmur of my prayers eventually lulled me into restless sleep. What a nightmare.

I woke the next morning to the quiet of an empty house. Frank and Lita were gone. Who knows where? It was all the same to me. I was alone. My back still hurt, but its cries were overridden by another body part—my growling stomach. I hadn't eaten a bite since lunch the day before. I staggered into the kitchen, but didn't get my hopes up. Experience taught me that place would be as food-free as the last time I was there, the night before. I looked anyway.

The well-practiced rituals of my life demanded that I seek something to eat. But wonder of wonders, a plate was sitting on the kitchen counter! It contained a hard-fried egg and an old biscuit. I remember the egg in particular; it had droplets of congealed grease on its dimpled surface. It was the most luscious-looking meal I had ever seen.

I grabbed the egg in my hand and shoved it into my mouth. I didn't chew. I swallowed it whole. I tried to apply the same treatment to the biscuit, but nearly broke a tooth. That sucker was hard as a baseball. I grabbed a table knife and began to chip away at the biscuit. I remember thinking: I can do this. It's just like chipping ice with a pick. In due course, the biscuit was in my stomach. All was well in the world, except for my sore back. I thought it would get better soon. It always did.

When Lita worked the day shift, things were all right at home. I saw people every day. I ate dinner at a normal time. Frank didn't go to the bar every night. He sulked and got shit-faced at home. Frank treated me a little better when Lita was around.

I wish things could have stayed that way, but they didn't. Lita got a new job at Lockheed Missiles and Space. But there was a problem; lots of earnest young people wanted to work for Lockheed. It was the Apple Computer of its day. Lockheed used its occupational desirability to great effect. They made their new employees jump through lots of hoops. Their discipline was legendary. You showed up on time, every day, or you got fired.

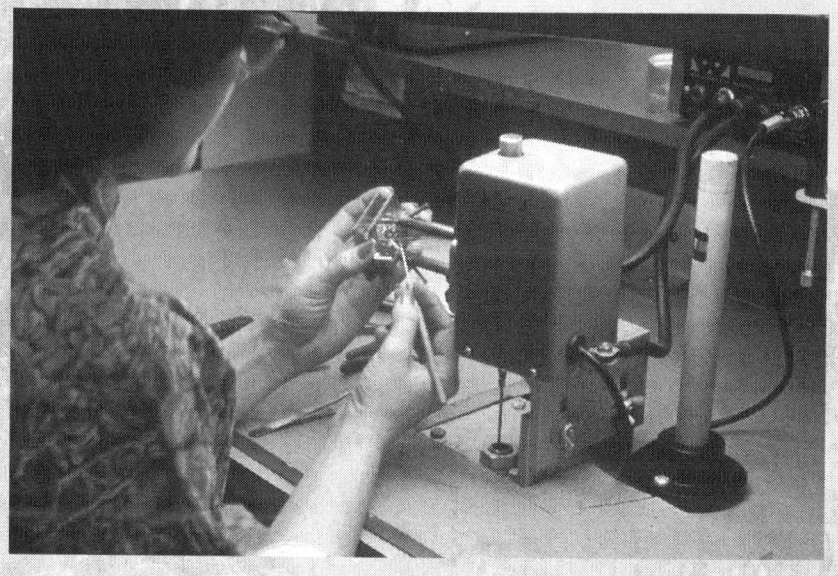

⬦⬦⬦

This personal family photograph is the only officially
sanctioned depiction of an electronics welder. Lita was one
of fewer than a dozen people in the world who accomplished
that task. The gold wires were welded because contemporary
solder joints would not take the extreme vibration and stress
of a missile launch. Lita was the last electronics welder.

Lita was required to work a lot of night shifts. That was okay with her. The night shift paid a premium. That was a necessary benefit for someone whose husband regularly spent his whole pay-check on strong drink and loose women. There was nothing new about what happened next. It was a small part of Lita and Frank's well-practiced suite of abusive behaviors. When Lita worked the night shift, Frank partied every night. I didn't eat dinner. Done deal; it worked out that way, 99 percent of the time.

I had to find ways to get my own dinner. None of those ways led to Faye Wolfe's front door. Faye barely had the resources to feed herself. The money for her irascible yardman and sullen housekeeper was provided by the person who was set to inherit Faye's house. The inheritor was just protecting Faye's only capital asset. It made perfect business sense.

It only took me a few days to realize I hadn't landed my much-desired regular job. That detail didn't matter to me. Faye and I were in love with each other. Not the carnal kind—the good kind. We had long conversations, almost every day. Faye Wolfe was the first person to provide me with unconditional love.

Frank was a sucker for door-to-door salesmen—if they could catch him on a rare evening when he was drinking at home. The first traveling salesman arrived the night after we moved into the Senter Road house. He sold Frank a Kirby vacuum cleaner that cost as much as a late-model car ("Just five dollars a week for a million weeks"). Other salesmen sold Frank brushes, kitchen gadgets, more magazines than I can remember—and a photo shoot. The resultant pictures from that session cost over $400 in 1962, not including the exorbitantly priced reprints Lita bought. Lita and Frank were both driving cars that should have been in the junkyard years before.

⬦⬦⬦

This photo is from the traveling salesman's shoot. It makes me want to puke. Everyone looks so cheerful. But Lita's smile doesn't reveal that she was working eighty hours per week to pay Frank's ever-growing bar tab. My smile doesn't reveal there was a 20 percent chance Frank had pulled me out of bed the night before and beat me up. Frank wears the only honest smile in this photograph. That man was getting all the strange pussy he wanted and buying rounds for the house almost every night at the Rock Castle bar.

Here's the important photo from the 1962 photo set Frank and Lita bought from a door-to-door photographer. Lita hand-tinted the black-and-white original to create a color masterpiece. This photo became Frank and Lita's logo, their emblem. Everyone in the family had a hand-tinted, expensively framed copy of this photo on their side table. Lita refused to pack the original photo with the family goods during our frequent moves. She said, "I want to keep that sucker safe." So why is this heirloom cracked? Because Lita sailed it across the room and missed Frank's forehead only because he drunkenly stumbled away from the solid brass frame's spinning trajectory. It made for great theater, just like always. So was added another member of Lita's curse-photo collection.

◇◇◇

Main curse photo from the 1962 photo set Frank and Lita bought from a door-to-door photographer. This photo once depicted Frank, Lita, and me, but Lita carefully tore off and burned all of Frank's portion and most of hers. The tear didn't touch any portion that includes me. From a witch's perspective that is very important; photo tears are powerful curses. My mother didn't want to hurt me. Poor Lita wasn't a good enough witch to see that she left the most important curse intact, torn right through the middle of her face. She should have used scissors. Any half-decent witch knows that.

◇◇◇

Lita stayed with her sap for the summer and fall of 1964
for a simple reason; he had this Crown Imperial with
a huge backseat, and lots of money, and he allowed
Lita to spend it on good times and pretty things.

10

WORKING MORE/STILL POOR

I went to Faye's house after school and on weekends. I noted the condition of her garden as I walked down the pathways. I never failed to see things that needed improvement, areas that needed cleaning. I knew I could safely pick the litter but make no improvement to the landscape. I couldn't pull a single weed. Eli had them memorized. In fact, he left weeds standing to see if I would pull them. There would have been hell to pay if he caught me working in Faye's garden, and she would have paid the price.

I walked up to the side door. I paused and noted the ancient artifacts that were scattered around. I never grew tired of seeing them. I knocked on the door. It took Faye a long time to grunt and shuffle up. She struggled with the ancient bolt. I heard Faye swearing and apologizing in equal measure on the other side of the door. She didn't like to keep me waiting. I didn't mind. It gave me time to collect my thoughts, to get ready for our visit. Like I was seeing a date.

In due course, the door swung open. Faye stood to one side and tried to say hello. But the pain and exertion of leaving the bed and opening the door removed most of the joy from that greeting. Faye winced and grimaced. She was barely upright, but she refused my offer of support.

I leaned in and gave her a hug. I automatically looked around the room and checked the status of its equipment. Was the wood box full? Was the stove lit? It usually wasn't. I asked Faye, "Do you want a fire?"

She always responded with the same line, "I'm not that cold." That was pure bullshit. It was generally cold enough to hang meat in the cottage. Faye didn't want a fire because she believed it was like burning money. When she had the money to buy wood, she didn't have the energy to feed the fire. Even if Faye didn't need to heat the house, I fired the stove. I wanted Faye to have hot water for a little while.

The stove was an eternally hungry beast. Its round lids were like the gaping maws of baby birds; they were never satisfied. Faye's stove was always calling for wood. The construction scraps that Eli sold to Faye were easy to cut and split, but they burned like paper. The large wood box emptied with amazing rapidity. Keeping it filled remained my chief job at Faye's house.

Faye eventually trusted me enough to do some of her grocery shopping. That was a big step. She had given one of my schoolmates a twenty-dollar bill and a grocery list. She never saw the boy again. Faye bitterly said, "I went hungry for two weeks because of that little shit."

I believed Faye's story. That kid watched me come out of Thrifty drugstore with a half-gallon of butter brickle ice cream. He stepped directly into my path and provided me with a grim greeting: "I saw you buy that ice cream. I know you've got over nine dollars in your pocket. Give it to me or I'll beat you up."

I replied automatically, like I was a robot, "My stepfather was a marine-trained drill sergeant. If I come home without the change, he will beat me up worse than you. So go ahead and hit me. At least I'll have some marks to show I put up a fight."

I braced myself to receive a beating. The other kid was taller and stronger than I. But an unexpected thing happened. Instead, the mugger slumped his shoulders and looked down at the ground and paused for a second. Like he was remembering something. He looked deflated. The mugger spun on his heels and ran off into the night.

But I didn't cheat Faye. Not a penny. I was her go-to guy and all-around friendly helper. When I was done with my chores, I sat with Faye. When she felt bad, we had bedside visits. I watched TV with her. I wanted to watch The Three Stooges show. Faye didn't. She said, "I suffered through those idiots thirty years ago, I don't need to go through that again."

When Faye felt better, we sat at her kitchen table. That is where our best visits occurred. Faye asked about my life and what I was doing. I never told Faye the truth about my home life. I believed things were as they should be. It was my normal. Then there was the important part: I was programmed to automatically spew the false storylines that were provided by Frank and Lita. My willingness to do so was pragmatic. I didn't want to run the chance that Frank would hear any negative reportage. He would have beaten the hell out of me.

After Faye had several ounces of whiskey in her, she loosened up. That's when she told her stories. I loved them. She told me old stories and new ones. I heard the same ones, over and again. I didn't mind hearing them. I just wanted to be with someone who liked me.

Faye loved to reminisce about her grand times. She wanted to relive them. That was the Faye part of her name. Sadly, her stories always ended with the Mariah part—a crippled old lady who spent her days and nights sitting alone in a cold house.

Faye and I cried a lot during our visits. I knew why she cried. I didn't know why I was crying. I thought I was being a baby. I didn't understand my tears for another half century. The book writing process explained them to me. Tears notwithstanding, I was pleased to have a friend.

But I wasn't looking for a friend when I met Faye. I was looking for a steady job. I still wanted to earn money so I could buy things. That wasn't going to happen with Faye. She seldom paid me anything. When she did, I felt guilty. I loved Faye with all my heart, but I still needed a job.

The revelation of my true status with Faye coincided with another vocational epiphany; I finally realized that the lawn mowing gig wasn't going to provide me with a stable income. Too many other earnest young boys had mowers, time, and experience. I also determined that folks who didn't mow their own lawns are a fickle breed. They loved my work one week but didn't want me the next.

I branched out in my money-making ventures. Everybody had rose plants growing in their yard. Most seemed to be unpruned. I pruned a few plants here and there around the neighborhood and received no complaints. That changed when I pruned a farm wife's garden. I'll never forget how pleased she looked as she walked past her newly pruned roses.

She stopped in her tracks when she passed a plant of Margo Koster. I had whacked the former two-foot plant down to about four inches. That seemed to be the right thing to do. She leaned forward on her cane, looked disapprovingly at the tiny stubs, and spoke in a quavering voice, "Young man, did you know it took that plant thirty years to get that big?"

✧✧✧

My sixteen-year-old self standing in front of Lita's rose plants. Duet is the large rose plant behind me. Lita paid $18.50 for this plant when it first came out in 1961. That was almost a week's pay for her. Lita worked more overtime to make up the shortfall. Exactly twenty years later, I discovered my first rose mutation on another Duet plant. I named the mutation Loeta Liggett. San Jose, California, 1966.

◇◇◇

When I was twelve, someone paid me to remove these
formerly overgrown pelargoniums. I pruned and replanted
them in our front yard. San Jose, California, 1963.

I wasn't allowed near the farm wife's roses again. But that eventuality was not entirely my fault; her husband sold the farm to developers. Tacky ghetto homes replaced her rose beds before the next pruning season came along.

My hunger and desperation forced me to seek other fiscal avenues. I knocked on people's doors and asked if I could clean their bathrooms. I had a lot of experience with that job. I had been cleaning Lita's bathrooms for years. My mother saw that job as being a way to train me for life. But she found a way to inject a radically feminist monologue to the job.

"My mother didn't make my brothers do housework," she said. "They all said it was girls' work. That kind of shit ain't gonna fly around here, Tommy. Get your fuckin' ass in there and clean that bathroom." So it was that I became an ace bathroom cleaner when I was six.

I soon discovered a stone-cold fact. Aside from my mother, few other women would allow a ragamuffin into their homes for any reason. They certainly didn't want me in their holy of holies, the bathroom.

But I did get one taker on my cleaning offer. A wonderful older woman allowed me to clean her bathroom. But she hovered over me while I scrubbed. I could tell she didn't really trust me to do the work. After I finished, she fed me a wonderful lunch. She served blackberry swirl ice cream. I had no idea such a flavor existed. I appreciated the filling lunch. Rations continued to be a hit-or-miss proposition in Frank and Lita's house.

When the nice lady set lunch in front of me, her real objective was revealed; she had brought me into her home for conversation. She was lonely. The nice lady told me about her long and glorious life. After lunch, she showed me the furniture she had picked up in her travels around the world. It was the stuff of oriental dreams, hand-carved mahogany fantasies that were fit for an emperor. Dragons and phoenixes carved in deep relief on ancient hardwood. Jade sculptures and ivory balls. A silk cushion that once bore the imprint of a princess's ass.

It was all great stuff. It made for a wonderful tour. But I was thinking, aw shit, Tommy. This woman wants to become another Faye Wolfe to you. Please don't take that last sentence the wrong way. I loved my time with Faye. I liked doing her chores. But I didn't need another needy person of like kind to suck the hours out of my days and nights. I already had one lonely old woman who needed a steady inrush of time and emotion. Beyond that, I didn't see much future in working for another impoverished old lady.

I was in a pickle. I still needed a job. But where would I find it? I was far too young to get a work permit. Any job I found would be illegal, an under-the-table proposition.

There weren't many venues for work in our area. Our new suburban neighborhood was located several miles from San Jose's center. Businesses were few and far between. An ocean of new homes stood on one side of Senter Road. Scattered islands of farm-land were on the other.

I tried speaking with the orchardists to see if they had regular work, but they all seemed to have some guy hanging around who had worked for them since about 1918. Those dudes didn't want a passing boy to horn in on the action—especially the easy farm jobs that could be done by someone who weighed just seventy-five pounds.

The few orcharding jobs I was offered were the kind that wore out adult males. I tried to pick cherries but failed when it was determined I couldn't haul a "short" twelve-foot, eighty-pound tripod ladder on my right shoulder. I was willing to try, but the farmer said, "I don't want to get in trouble because I allowed some damned-fool kid to take a header off a cherry ladder and break his neck."

But the orchardist was good-natured about my shortcomings: "Come back next winter. After Christmas, when the leaves are off the trees. I need someone to dig around the base of the trees, about a foot down, all around. That exposes the bud union and roots to the frost. It kills the insect larvae and eggs."

In late December, I dutifully returned. The orchardist looked surprised to see me but went along with his part of the deal. He handed me a round-point shovel and said, "I'll give you ten cents a tree. Start with that one." He pointed to a massive Royal Anne cherry. It was more than fifty feet tall and as wide. It had the spread of a four-hundred-year-old valley oak. But that aspect of the tree's magnificence didn't matter to me. That monster was four feet thick at the base. The farmer expected me to dig a foot-deep trench all the way around the tree. If you're handy with math, that's about fourteen feet on the inside of the trench.

I stuck the shovel to make the first cut, but the orchardist placed his hand on my shoulder and stopped me. "These trees are old. They were planted by my grandfather. I want you to go easy on 'em. Don't smack the trunk. Don't nick the roots. Cherries ain't very forgiving. They'll get crown gall."

I dug and hacked at the mucky south San Jose clay. The orchardist returned at various times to check my progress and to ensure I was not damaging his tree. Finally, late in the afternoon, he left me alone. I finished digging around the tree not long after.

I stood, stretched my back, and picked up the shovel. I admired my handiwork. It looked just like the trees around me that had been dug by the farmer's adult helpers. I also noted that the farmer had made me dig around the largest tree in the orchard.

I trudged and stumbled back to the barn. The orchardist was sitting in a chair reading a newspaper. A few feet away, a fire was burning in a fifty-gallon drum. I recognized the smell—ancient cherry wood, the best firewood on earth. The orchardist casually looked up from his reading, "How many did ya dig?"

"Just one."

The orchardist stood, stretched, and placed the newspaper on the chair seat. "Well, that's one more than I expected a wimpy-looking twelve-year-old kid to dig." The orchardist pulled a dime out of his pocket and handed it to me. "Come back tomorrow. I've got 500 more trees waiting for you." The orchardist seemed to think he had cracked a joke, because he began to laugh. He was slapping his hands on his knees.

I murmured a quiet thank you and walked away. I found my bicycle and rode the long mile home.

11

MARTIAN LIVING IN A TIN CAN

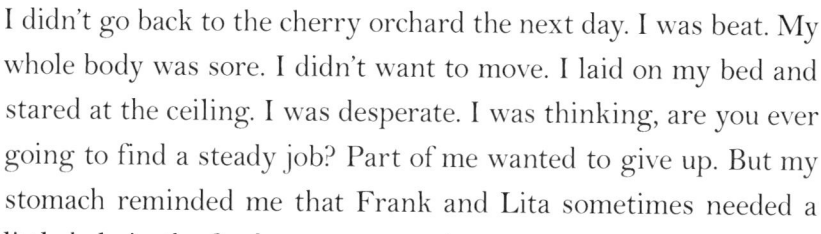

I didn't go back to the cherry orchard the next day. I was beat. My whole body was sore. I didn't want to move. I laid on my bed and stared at the ceiling. I was desperate. I was thinking, are you ever going to find a steady job? Part of me wanted to give up. But my stomach reminded me that Frank and Lita sometimes needed a little help in the food procurement department.

I rode my bicycle farther and farther in a fruitless quest to satisfy that need. In my small mind, it looked as if I were following one of the mirages that we saw on our trips to Texas. Even the thirstiest cowboy knew the folly of chasing those fantasies.

I was just about ready to give up on my quest, but providence smiled upon me. I was picking litter around Faye's house. It drove her crazy to see the refuse of other people's lives blow into her garden. I took a moment to rest from that never-ending job. I was bored. I felt lazy. I was dawdling. I didn't want to retrieve the Budweiser can that was stuck in the middle of Faye's largest cholla cactus.

I stood and looked off into the west. I noted the mobile home park on the other side of the mountain road. My grandmother lived in a trailer park. She had lived in a lot of them. I stayed in some of them too. That knowledge enabled me to accurately rate the trailer park next to Faye's property; it was ratty looking. That place was the final resting place for hundreds of run-down coaches from the 1930s, '40s, and '50s. The tiny yards were overgrown and strewn with junk. It was an eyesore. That was the main reason I had never bothered to give the place a closer look.

But I was bored enough that day to stare at anything, so I allowed my eyes to linger on the trailer park. I noted an ancient sign by the entrance. It bore the trailer park's name in faded letters. I had ridden by that sign hundreds of times without really seeing it. Then I saw another sign, a few feet away. It was smaller, but more tasteful. It read: Gosseling Printing. I thought, wow! That company might need some help. They might give me a job.

I hurried through Faye's list of chores. I gave her a kiss on the cheek and ran outside. I jumped on my bicycle and rode to the trailer park driveway. I paused for a moment. I remember thinking, these people don't want to hire a kid. There's nothing here for you. But something inside of me said, ride on. There is promise.

I gathered my courage and rode into the trailer park. But I was perplexed. Was there really a printshop in the middle of this endless collection of junky house trailers? Was a larger building hidden inside? I slowly rode up and down the roads that wound through the park. I didn't see a building.

I finally rode back toward the main entrance and turned on the first side street. I stopped at a trailer and parked my bike. I walked up to the door and knocked. A nice older woman answered the door. She gave me a cheerful, "Good afternoon."

I said, "Pardon me for bothering you, but the sign out on the road says there is a printshop in here, but I couldn't find it."

The woman's expression changed at the mention of the print-shop. Her face darkened. I thought she was going to explode. She jabbed her finger back in the direction I had traveled and said, "Over there. That crazy old bastard lives over there." The woman glared at me and slammed the door.

I stood in front of the woman's trailer for a moment. I was perplexed. I thought, what did I do to her? I was about to leave when the door flew open again. The woman yelled, "And if you find that old sonofabitch at home, tell him to stop making such a goddamned racket. It's getting to be where a person can't get any sleep around here." She slammed the door so hard the trailer's windows rattled.

I stood in the driveway for a moment. I was somewhat confused by the vehemence of the woman's response to my inquiry. I remember thinking that woman didn't think much of the man who runs the printshop. Maybe he's a nut or a pervert. Maybe I'd better ride on out of here and seek work somewhere else.

But again, my inner muse came to the rescue by urging me on. I turned and looked in the direction that was indicated by the irate woman's finger jabs. I didn't see a printshop. I saw a thirty-six-foot Spartan house trailer.

Now, some of you might be getting skeptical by now. You might be wondering how a twelve-year-old boy could tell a thirty-six-foot Spartan from an aardvark. Yes, I could. My grandmother owned an identical trailer. It was her pride and joy, until she traded it in for a newer, larger Spartan. I knew those trailers inside and out. My relatives had spent the previous five years bragging about the salient points of Spartan house trailers. Why? They were built of solid, aircraft-grade aluminum alloy. Spartan trailers were tough. They were durable. They were tiny.

◇◇◇

I'm on the left in this photo, standing in front of my
grandmother's ancient Spartan trailer. Please note the
expression on my face. I was in the middle of a good book
and wanted to see how it finished. I certainly didn't want
to be interrupted just so my grandmother could take
a silly old photograph. The other people aren't worth
naming, so I won't. China Lake Naval Air Station, 1957.

They were skinny, airplane-like metal tubes that contained lots of well-designed, miniature rooms. I figured there couldn't be a printshop in that thing.

This was a real come-to-Jesus moment for me. I had been looking for the printshop for about fifteen minutes. I was ready to give up. But I hadn't eaten a decent meal in a few days. I was hungry. That consideration provided reason enough for me to contact the folks who ran the printshop.

I walked my bike across the road. I stopped in front of the Spartan trailer. When I looked a little closer, I noted a small, well-made sign. It read: Gosseling Printing. I had found the printshop. And then I thought there wouldn't be room enough to print much in that tin can. They probably didn't need a helper.

I was about to turn away, but my stomach growled. I said to myself, you're here. Just knock on the damned door. They'll say no and you can go home. You can say you gave it your best shot.

I parked the bike and walked up the steps to the trailer's small porch. I knocked on the door. In a few seconds, the door slammed backward on its hinges. I almost jumped off the porch. An angry old man stepped into the doorway and loudly declaimed, "Whatever you're selling, I don't want any. Go away."

I couldn't walk away. My feet were frozen to the porch. Why? I was transfixed by the apparition that loomed above me. He looked to be a hundred years old. He was six feet two and rail thin, but muscular. He had huge, calloused hands with large, dirty, cracked fingernails.

But my eyes didn't linger on those details for long, I was staring at the man's head. It was huge, with a bulbous top. He was bald as an egg. I remember thinking, this guy looks like the Martians I see in comic books, maybe even like a mad scientist.

The old man startled me out of my thoughts when he barked, "Well, kid, I ain't got all day. What do ya want? Spit it out."

I said, "I'm looking for a job. I want to work. I need the money."

The expression on the angry giant's face softened a little. He gazed into the distance and blinked his eyes. He looked as if he was remembering something. The man smiled and stuck out his hand and said, "I'm Max. Max Gosseling. Who are you?"

"I'm Tom Liggett. But most people call me Tommy."

Max said, "You don't look like you could work very hard. You look like the type who thinks about girls all the time."

That wasn't the response I was expecting from a prospective employer. I had no idea where he got that idea. Girls were alien creatures to me. Icky, even. Why would I think about them? But I forged on. "I'm a hard worker. Give me a chance."

Max rubbed his hand over his head as he spoke, "Well, I guess so. But I ain't gonna pay ya much. I'll give ya a nickel an hour for every year of your life. How old are ya anyway, kid?"

I said, "I'm twelve. Wait—you'll really pay me sixty cents an hour?"

Max said, "Yeah, yeah, I'll pay ya, if ya last. Lookin' at you, I don't think ya will. But my last kid took a powder on me. I got a big job in here that needs finishing. Come on in."

I stepped through the front door of the ancient Spartan trailer. This one wasn't anything like my grandmother's trailer of similar vintage. Her coach was like a dollhouse. It was lined with acres of gleaming wood and polished chrome. My grandmother's house was neat as a pin.

Max Gosseling's trailer was a rat's nest. It was filled with all his possessions. He lived in the place. It also contained a mad collection of unidentifiable stuff.

Tommy Tomlinson, my grandmother's third
husband, in front of his brand-new 1959 Spartan
trailer. He had reason to feel proud; he just bought
the finest full-sized house trailer ever built.

Max waved his arm and walked away from me. "Come on, kid. I'll give you a quick tour. You don't want to get lost in here." Max laughed as he cracked that joke, but I could tell he was proud of his pint-sized industrial enterprise.

He led me to the rear of the trailer. It contained a large-format photography studio, several hand-operated letterpresses, a modern lithographic press, and innumerable cases of lead type. Strange implements and chemical cans were scattered everywhere. The place smelled like an oil refinery.

Max led me toward the front of the trailer, then stopped at a side door. "The bathroom's in here." I stuck my head in the door and recoiled. The place smelled worse than any cowboy outhouse I had ever encountered. The rotten linoleum was saturated with urine and who-knows-what. The sink was encapsulated in lime and grime. It was stained an ugly black/brown/green color from years of accumulated soap and printer's ink.

But those items just provided the overture. The main star of that bathroom freak show was the toilet. It was encapsulated in shit. I'm not exaggerating. The outside of the toilet was covered by years of an old man's ass-dribbles and near misses. Shit stalactites ran down the front of the bowl. Stark visual and olfactory evidence indicated that the front of the tank also received its share of collateral shitting.

But that was just the introduction to the main theme. The toilet bowl was a bona fide horror story. It was covered with a solid inch of shit. Not gooey-runny shit. Hard shit. Like rock. The sloping mass ran well below the current water line in places. It was a shit sculpture of magnificent proportions.

Some people might wonder about the process that created a scatological confection of that scale. I soon determined that fact, but I'll share the secret ahead of time: Max ate a high-fiber diet. Lots of cabbage, carrots, and apples. It gave him a continual case of the runny, exploding shits. Every time Max parked his skinny ass on the toilet, he infused it with shit spray. The spray dried on the upper surfaces of the seat and toilet bowl. When he stood up, it dribbled off his ass and went all over the bathroom.

Now, I've got to be honest here. I walked into that trailer print-shop with a growling stomach. That consideration made me believe I was willing to do anything to get cheeseburger money. But my brain and nose were doing all they could to override my stomach's driving need. I didn't like the direction this job prospect was leading me. I thought, aw hell, he's gonna make me clean that sonofabitch.

Max snapped me out of my toilet-staring gaze. He said, "Well, come on kid, stop daydreaming, the tour's over. I gotta get this job finished and delivered."

Once I was clear of the bathroom, I breathed a sigh of relief. There would be no industrial-strength toilet cleaning for Tommy. At least for today.

I followed Max to the front of the trailer. A small mattress was laid across the very front of the trailer. A portable tabletop stretched over the bed. I noted an odor as I walked toward the table. It was coming from the mattress. The smell of mildew and old man sweat. More animal-like than human. Not rank, but pervasive.

The table was set for work. Stacks of paper and pots of rubber cement stood in orderly rows.

Max told me to sit at the table. He explained the job of the day. Max printed advertisement and postcards. My job was to glue a postcard to the sheet. The ad was in black and white. The post-card was in vivid color. The images were photographs. They were highlighted by artistic text with flowing letters.

Max beamed as he handed me the first postcard. "That's living color, kid. It's the new thing. Black and white's on its way out." The modern era is full of color images. They are everywhere. But it hadn't always been that way. Until the mid-1960s, the bulk of print and video images were in black and white.

In due course, I finished gluing Max's brochures. He provided grudging approval that I had accomplished the task to a minimum standard. It was time to get on to the next task—packing the brochures for delivery. Max did that the old-fashioned way; he wrapped them in packages. Max showed me how to tear the thick, glossy paper off a four-foot-wide roll. I ran gummed sealing tape across an ancient marble water wheel to wet the dry adhesive.

I completed the first package. Max looked over my shoulder and barked, "Kid, that package is so lumpy, it looks like you wrapped a sack of potatoes. I sell printing, not spuds! Do it again!"

My second attempt at package wrapping was better than the first. Max grunted his approval. I wrapped the rest of the printing order and carried it to his car.

Max prepared his dinner while I loaded the printing order in the car. He ate the same meal three times a day, seven days a week. Max opened a battered old pressure cooker. He placed a half-pound cube of raw hamburger on the bottom. He placed a potato and an apple on top. A cow-sized wedge of cabbage and two carrots went in last. Max put the pressure cooker on the stove. He had the operation timed perfectly. Max's dinner was done just as I loaded the last package.

Max turned away from the stove and stuck his hand in a trouser pocket. He deftly counted out my wages, then placed the last coin in my hand with a flourish. Max offered me his hand and smiled. "Give me your phone number. I'll let you know when

⬥⬥⬥

I helped Max create thousands of these promotional calendars in 1964. It was a lot of work. I wrapped the finished calendars in large bundles with heavy, enamel-coated paper. That stuff would cut human skin like a razor. The simple-appearing postcard on top is a thing of beauty; Max ran it through his Davidson Davalith printer five times on one side and two on the other. The registration (color matching) is perfect. Years later, I showed printers this card; they couldn't believe the quality of Max Gosseling's work—he was the best of them all.

The back side of Max's wonderful postcard. It is a perfect example of the printer's art.

◇◇◇

The back side of Max's calendar. No one could match his prices. He just wanted to stay busy.

HI-FI COLOR

You Need It — We Have It!

Direct Mail Advertising

– For –

Motels . . . Restaurants . . . Hotels
Product Manufacturers and Jobbers
Retail Store Announcements
Service Stations . . . Automobile Dealers

Business Cards — Business Reply Cards
Post Cards — Giant Cards — Panoramics
Folders — all sizes — printed on 10 pt. Kromekote Stock

For more information — write or call

max gosseling

4210 Monterey Road · San Jose, Calif.

Tel. 225-2732

Always FIRST in Color

PLACE STAMP HERE

POST CARD

Address

POST CARDS · PRINTS · BROCHURES

For *Living Color* POST CARDS

Tel. 225-0176

max gosseling

4010 SOUTH FIRST
SAN JOSE, CALIF.

I need you again." I quickly gave him my phone number. Max shooed me out the door.

The door slammed behind me as I walked down the steps. I turned and looked at Max's trailer. I reflected on the whirlwind events of the past few hours. I thought about Max Gosseling. He was firm, but fair. He didn't yell at me or get weird. He paid me the promised amount, to the penny.

The money was great. I knew I would eat that night. But I was more pleased about another aspect—I knew I had found a steady job. I had been searching for that treasure for over a year. I felt empowered. I could regularly buy books, magazines, records, sheet music, plant seeds, miniature electric motors, and candy bars. I could buy food when Frank and Lita didn't bring home the groceries. I was exhilarated. I rode straight to the burger joint and enjoyed my new freedom. I realized I was no longer entirely dependent upon anyone else's efforts to fill my stomach.

A few days later, Max called me. He said, "Kid, I need help with a rush job. Come over right now." I rode my bike to Max's trailer. He was out front. The trunk of his 1964 Ford Thunderbird was open. Without preamble, he pointed at the car. "Kid. There's a bag in the trunk. Bring it over here."

I walked over to the car. A fifty-pound bag of forest mulch sat crosswise in the trunk. I recognized the product. It was a popular brand. I struggled to lift the bag out of the high trunk sill, but finally managed. Max noted my difficulty. "Kid. Don't tear the bag. We need it to be in one piece."

That statement puzzled me. I had used countless bags of garden products. Their use was similar. You tore the bag and dumped its contents on the ground or into a wheelbarrow. The bag went into the trash. I wondered why this guy wanted the bag. I did not voice any of those concerns. I needed the money.

I hugged the bag to my chest and struggled over to where Max was standing. He pointed to a spot on the edge of the lawn. "Put it over there, front side facing the sun." I accomplished this and stood back. The label stood out with stark relief in the late afternoon sun. Max barked, "Get out of the way! You're blocking my light!"

I turned and noticed that Max had a huge camera in his hand. He beamed when he saw me staring at it. "This is a large-format German camera. It cost as much as a car." Max snapped a half-dozen shots, lowered the camera, and said, "Follow me."

Max walked through the trailer door and turned left. He walked down the hall and stopped at the bathroom door. "Kid. I'm gonna show you this one time, because you need to know so you can be more help to me. Otherwise, you're not gonna be working this side of the operation."

Max pointed into the wretched bathroom and said, "Come in here."

Aw, Jesus, what's this crazy old fuck gonna do to me?

I reluctantly walked into the bathroom. The only thing that was the same about that place was the smell. Otherwise, the room had been transformed. A table was set across the toilet and shower area. It was covered with long pans. They looked like baking pans, but deeper. Strange implements were scattered about the tabletop. A huge timer took pride of place.

Max saw the questions on my face. "This is a darkroom. This is where I develop film."

Max unscrewed the lightbulb from the ceiling fixture. He replaced it with a dark-looking bulb. The contacts made a popping

◇◇◇

Max continually started and stopped the huge
timer, which took pride of place in the darkroom.
Max Gosseling's last darkroom. Circa 1969.

sound when they touched the lamp base. The replacement bulb produced deep, red light.

Max reached behind me and closed the bathroom door. He slid a dark curtain across the opening. Max said, "This place isn't designed for two people. It's gonna be tight in here. Stay out of the way and, whatever you do, don't open that door."

"Yes, sir."

Max opened bottles and dumped the contents into the pans. He explained the name and purpose of each chemical. Some of them produced acrid odors. The fumes brought welcome relief from the festering toilet between my feet.

Max opened the camera and removed the film. He put the film into the pans in an ordered sequence. He pushed the start button on the timer. He explained every step to me with patient grace. When that was done, he clipped the developed negative to a string. Max said, "We can't do anything more with this right now. It needs to dry. Go out and spread that bag of mulch around the yard."

I nodded my head and left the bathroom/darkroom. I was quite pleased to escape that place. I found a likely place to spread the mulch, disposed of the bag, and walked into the trailer.

Max noted my entrance. "Follow me." He went into the bathroom/darkroom and retrieved the just-developed negative. He placed the negative on a light box. Max carefully examined each negative with a magnifying device. He grunted his approval and picked the best. He used the negative to make a plate for his Davidson offset press. That operation required another trip into the bathroom/darkroom.

Max set up the press and printed a thousand brochures. Max set the printed brochures aside. He showed me how to clean the press. He ended that demonstration with a warning: "Kid, you're gonna clean that letterpress over there, but ya ain't gonna touch this one. If ya drop a rag inside, the press will be ruined." Max chased that concept with one that was quite chilling: "If ya get your hand caught between the rollers, it'll pull your arm off."

I shivered and thought, well, Tommy, you discovered something worse than cholla cactus to work around, didn't you?

Max grabbed the brochures and said, "Help me collate these." We went to the front room and sat at the work table. Two jars of rubber cement and a stack of postcards stood in the center. I sighed when I saw the postcards. This was a boring job.

Max sat down next to me. He grabbed a brochure and postcard. He deftly applied a tiny dab of rubber cement to the corners of the card. He attached the card to the brochure with scientific efficiency.

I could tell that Max also found the job to be boring and repetitive, because he talked more than usual. But it wasn't conversation of the normal kind. Max didn't ask questions about me. Some people might find that to be rude behavior. I believe that lack derived from Max's vast store of life experiences. He had a lot of stories to tell. Max also knew that skinny twelve-year-old boys didn't look for jobs unless they needed them. Max knew better than to ask leading questions. He might not like the answers.

Max told me he had a drunken, abusive father. "He worked me like a dog and beat me like a mule. When I turned eleven, I finally decided I had enough. I waited for my father out by the barn. When he came around the corner, I smacked him in the face with a flat shovel. Knocked him out cold. I looked him in the face and said, 'Take that, you bastard.' I walked away from home and didn't look back. I never spoke to the sonofabitch again."

Max's revelation surprised me. I couldn't imagine being on my own at such a young age. "But what did you do then, Max? I mean, how did you get food? Where did you sleep?"

Max surprised me with his response. "I enlisted in the marines as a drummer boy. I told them I was thirteen."

I said, "Wow! Cool!"

Max snorted and looked at me like I was an idiot-child. "It was rough, kid. I got out as soon as I could, in two years, when I really was thirteen. I found a man who was willing to take me on as a printer's devil. He didn't pay me nothin' at all, just room and board for working eighty hours a week."

Max smiled and looked at me as he spoke a final sentence: "That's what you are, kid, a printer's devil. God put you on earth to devil this poor printer." Max laughed at his joke. I didn't know what to say.

Few modern people have ever heard of a printer's devil. That's too bad. Printers always had helper apprentices known as devils. Those guys did everything around a printer's shop and yard that the printer didn't want to do—cleaning presses, breaking down type, melting lead, lugging reams of paper, wrapping orders, delivering orders, pulling weeds in the lot, and cleaning the toilet.

Not long after I began to work for Max, he decided "to go big-time in the printing business." Please allow me to translate that from Max-speak: He bought a larger trailer. It was a beauty: a fifty-five-foot-long, ten-foot-wide, almost new Marlette.

Max announced that professional press movers would transfer his beloved equipment from the old trailer into the new one. "But you and me are gonna move everything else. But first, we gotta clean up the old Spartan."

From my perspective, that appeared to be an impossible task. Max's old trailer was a wreck. It had minor damage from an electrical fire. The floors were bowed from the continual stress of bearing tons of printing presses, paper, and lead type. The bathroom floor was spongy from years of piss, shit, industrial-strength soap, and chemical spatters. The trailer smelled like printer's ink and a buffalo wallow.

None of those factors deterred Max Gosseling. "It's a Spartan, kid, built out of solid aluminum. Contractors haul these things around to off-road jobsites. Someone will want it. They'll pay top dollar."

Max Gosseling was an intelligent man. He knew that no one would buy a trailer with a shit-encrusted toilet. Most people would replace the toilet with a shiny new one. Not Max; he was tight-fisted with his money. He had another plan in mind. Max went to his kitchen drawer and pulled out a stainless-steel table knife. He handed me the knife with a flourish and said, "Kid. Clean the toilet. Make it shine."

I nodded my head and trudged off toward the bathroom. I dreaded this job more than any I had done before. In the past, I held my urine for hours so I wouldn't have to piss into Max's rancid toilet. When I couldn't hold it anymore, I stood back two feet in a vain effort to avoid the smell and look. But this was inescapable. I knew I was doomed to have a close, personal relationship with the thing.

I used the table knife to chip away flakes of Max-shit. That took four hours. I used a scouring pad and abrasive cleanser for another two hours. I spent every minute on my knees. Max didn't offer gloves or goggles. But six hours of horrid work paid off; Max's toilet gleamed. It was stained and water spotted, but clean, inside and out.

Max had been watching my progress, though he didn't offer any tips. I obviously knew more about toilet cleaning than he did.

He finally looked over my shoulder and announced, "Kid, that toilet is clean enough for anyone." I believed that statement was an exaggeration, but it was what I wanted to hear.

I stood up. My knees hurt. My back hurt. My hands were sore and cramped from grasping the skinny table knife. I was covered from head to toe with specks and globs of Max's shit. But I was happy. Why? Because Frank and Lita weren't feeding me much. I knew I would eat that night.

I stumbled into the kitchen and watched Max as he finished preparing his nightly meal. He turned away from the stove and placed my pay into my hand. I thanked him and ran down the porch stairs. I pedaled my bike to the hamburger joint. I placed my order and sat at one of the outside tables.

It took me a few minutes to figure out that people were pointing at me. Some held their noses and giggled. Up to that point, I hadn't noticed the odors that were wafting off my body. I was a little embarrassed when I discovered that fact, but didn't really care. Lita and Frank had been feeding me shit. I spent the day scraping shit. I was covered with shit. But I had a jumbo cheeseburger, fries, and a strawberry milkshake in front of me. I felt as if I was in a bed of roses.

I reflected upon the circumstances of my wonderful life as I enjoyed the burger. Things were going well. I had a great teacher in my new school. None of the local punks had threatened my life in the past few days. Lita worked the day shift, sometimes. That was a saving grace. I regularly got hot meals and some company. Frank wasn't beating me up more than once or twice a week. My pint-sized backyard plant research station was flourishing. My printer's devil job was going well. I worked for Max three or four times a week.

But Faye Wolfe was the real reason I was happy. My life revolved around Faye's love, house, yard, and stove. That needy little monster never seemed to get enough wood. Faye's shaded, uninsulated cottage never seemed to get warm except for our conversations at the iron table. She needed me, and I desperately needed her.

12

"NO PLACE THAT HAD HURRICANES OR GODDAMNED SNOW"

I rushed home from school every day. I dropped off my books and musical instruments, then went to see Faye. Some days, I had very little time to spend with her. Maybe I had weeds to pull at home. Maybe I needed to practice an important musical part. Perhaps Max Gosseling had a rush job he needed to complete.

On those days, I lit Faye's stove, kissed her on the cheek, and hurried away. Faye was always disappointed when I didn't stay to visit. I was the lone bright spot in her life. Truth be told, I felt bad when I didn't spend more time with Faye. Part of that sentiment came from guilt. I was raised to believe that every bad thing in the world was my fault. I was a guilt-driven child.

But I missed Faye's company when I was busy. She was my only true friend. I spent as much time with Faye as I could. Our visits became ordered things. Not formal, structured. I lit Faye's stove and asked if she had chores. She usually had something or other for me to do. When all else failed, I gathered trash and pulled weeds in the garden. The latter activity was made possible by my age and experience. I was no longer afraid of Eli's reaction to my garden help. I discovered he was all bark and no bite. Faye never failed to warn me away from the cholla cactus and its lethally fine thorns. That, too, was part of our routine.

When I was done with my chores, I sought Faye. She was always in one of three places: the bathroom, in bed, or sitting at her kitchen table. The latter place was full of symbolic intent. When Faye sat there, she wanted to visit. I didn't always want to visit. I was a little boy. A boy who was full of plans and plants, books and mechanical toys. Cats and dogs. Music of my own making and that of my betters. Creek-side idylls and hikes on the mountain that spread above and away from our house.

I did my best to hide my disappointment when I wanted to be somewhere other than sitting with an old lady in a faded room. But Faye was always able to see through my screen. She said, "You rush along now. You don't need to spend so much time with an old woman." Faye looked downcast at those moments. Alone. That statement seldom failed to remind me about Faye's place in my life. I slid onto the bench and asked, "Would you like me to mix you a highball?"

That question brought back Faye's smile. "Yes, of course. But not too strong."

My reply was as formal as her request, "Oh. Of course not." I kept my true feelings about Faye's alcoholic serving size to myself. I was raised by a drunk. I watched people drink at every social gathering I attended, but never saw anyone who could down as much alcohol in one go as Faye Wolfe. She preferred a single, very large drink.

I walked into the kitchen and filled a tumbler with about six ounces of cheap whiskey and two ounces of flat soda water. No ice. Faye didn't have a functional freezer.

I filled an identical tumbler with water for me. No whiskey.

I placed the drinks on the table. Faye always said the same thing: "Oh, my. You mixed me such a strong drink. I don't think I can finish this." The first time she said that, I replied, "Oops! I messed up. Would you like me to pour the whiskey back into the bottle?"

Faye got a horrified expression on her face and said, "Oh, my, no, no, NO! That is bad luck. A curse. Don't ever pour liquor back into the bottle, Tommy." Ah, Faye, my girl, you knew all the rules of parties, strong drink, and curses, didn't you?

Faye began our conversations with a question about me. That was quite welcome. I spent much of my free time with the always-irascible Max Gosseling. He only talked about himself, if he talked at all.

Faye's inquiries about me opened the flood gates. I told her about everything in my life. She was horrified about some of my activities. Like when I got an expensive electromechanical toy for Christmas. I dismantled it the very next day. I wanted to get my hands on the tiny but powerful electric motor inside. It was better than the one that came with my erector set. Faye was terrified when I mentioned I had ridden my bike off a cliff. I carefully explained the lesson I learned from that experience; my Schwinn Corvette was not intended for off-road use. Faye broke down in tears when I told her about the bike fiasco.

I learned to keep that kind of secret to myself. I didn't like to see Faye cry. But my efforts in that direction didn't help much. Faye cried a lot during our visits. But I also noted an important detail about our visits—Faye laughed more than she cried. In my mind, that made our conversations worthwhile. They allowed her to relive the grand old times, when she was young, beautiful, and popular.

Faye revealed the fine details of her story in snippets. An anecdote here. A saying there. Maybe a line from an old song. Sometimes she matched her memories to photographs. That cemented them in my memory. Faye told the same stories, over and again. That was great. I didn't mind. But I tried to steer Faye into another direction. I wanted to hear all of her story, not just the highlights. That took a while.

Faye matched her stories to my age. It was a progressive thing. When I was eleven, the stories were fun and vague. Kid stuff. The stories grew in scope and detail as I aged. When I turned fifteen, Faye said, "You're not a little boy anymore. I can go a little deeper now." That was fine with me. I had a lot of questions, especially the big one: "Please, Faye, tell me what happened after the hurricane."

That question made Faye shiver, but she picked up the story where we had left off.

I was bruised, battered, and hungry. The fine clothes and jewelry I had accumulated were all gone. Thank god I had some photographs stashed with a friend back east, or they would be gone too. All I had was the clothes on my back, a new pair of boots, and an empty stomach. I got the hell out of Galveston.

I was nineteen, gorgeous, and curvy. I always found a nice man who was willing to pay the freight. I didn't know where I was headed when I left Galveston, except that it wasn't going to be anyplace that had hurricanes or goddamned snow. I had enough of that in South Dakota.

Faye took a long drink and stared at the tabletop. I could read her expressions quite easily by then. She tried to decide whether or not she should reveal a scandalous detail to me. Faye raised her chin and looked me in the eye. "I was raised in a boomtown. I passed through about ten of 'em before I ever went to Galveston."

My face took on a quizzical expression as I opened my mouth to ask a question, but Faye cut me off with a declaration: "I needed boomtowns to supply the nicer things in life. But America changed in 1900, Tommy. The West was closed. There was only one boom-town left: San Francisco."

Faye laughed and said, "You know they don't have hurricanes there, don't you?" Faye knew how to deliver a great punch line. She knew how to entertain a young man.

Faye removed her glasses and wiped away the mist that had been created by her laughter. She took a long pull from her drink and sat still for a while. She was composing herself. Like an actress who was preparing to go onstage.

It didn't take me long to bounce back from the Galveston fiasco. A few days later, I was in San Francisco, living in a fine hotel. Nineteen-year-old beauties were as popular then as they are now. But that kind of woman was easier to rent for an evening, back then. I did great in San Francisco. I had it made.

Things got even better for me over the next six years. I was living in the Palace Hotel. It was the nicest place in town. In San Francisco I had more clothes and jewels than ever before. The famous Italian opera star Enrico Caruso was staying there too. I know that because a man I knew

tried to get me to see a performance. I refused. I didn't
have anything against Caruso. I heard his recordings. He
was okay. I just couldn't stand the scraping of the violins
as they sawed back and forth, back and forth.

Faye paused her telling for a moment and did a great panto-
mime of a bad violin player. I started to laugh, but didn't make a
comment. I spent hours each day playing classical music on the
French horn and trumpet. I listened to classical music. It was the
one subject on which Faye and I disagreed.

Truth be told, my friend didn't care about high-toned
music. He wanted to walk into the opera house with the
prettiest girl in town on his arm. My friend didn't take
my refusal very well. He said he'd go find a girl who
was more grateful for what he did for her and stormed
out of my room.

I was glad to see the back of his head going out the
door. I was sick of him. He was like a lot of guys I knew.
They were all sweet, generous, and slow when they were
courting, but they were cheap and quick once they had you.
But there was a silver lining in that sometimes. When a
guy was a bad lover, quick was better.

I blushed when Faye said that. But the sentiment was not for-
eign to me. My mother and her female associates were always
teasing me about sex. Some of them were graphic in their ministrations. When they thought I wasn't listening, they talked about
three-minute men, quickie jerks, and premature ejaculators.

Faye laughed, "I have embarrassed you again."

"Oh, no. It's all right. It's kind of fun. Please go on."

After my friend stormed off, I decided to call it a night. I had been to a lot of parties in the previous days. I just wanted to rest. I was asleep in my room. First thing I knew, I got thrown out of bed, across the room, and onto the floor. The whole place was shaking. Stuff was crashing around, and the light fixture dropped from the ceiling. It was dark, I couldn't see anything. I was getting shaken around like a rat in a terrier's mouth.

It frightened hell out of me. I thought I was going to die. Out in the hall, some damned fool was screaming, "Get out, get out, the building's gonna collapse." I believed that idiot and ran down the stairs, out into the street. I was wearing just a house coat and slippers.

I stood outside for the longest time. It was cold as hell. Thank god some man gave me his overcoat. Otherwise I would have frozen to death. After a while, I could see the building wasn't going to fall. I mean, stuff was shaken loose all over, but the building was still standing. I decided to go back into the hotel, to get my things. I wasn't ready for what I saw inside.

The place was a madhouse. People were yelling and screaming. I saw two guys fighting in the hall. It took me a long time to climb five flights of stairs. The heel busted off my slipper before I got to the top. I kicked the blister-making sonofabitches and finally made it back to my room.

The door was standing open. I ran in and saw that the place was a shambles. All my boxes were open. This wasn't just earthquake damage. Someone had tossed my room. I looked around for my jewelry box. I kept all my good stuff in one place. But the box was gone; someone had taken the whole thing. My money was gone too. I looked around the room. It was knee-deep in spilled undergarments and fancy dresses. I just stood there with my fists clenched, shouting, Damn! Damn! Damn!

But I refused to cry. I was used to flying high, then getting smashed down to the ground. I was living up to my accursed middle name. It was a Mariah moment.

Anyway, it wasn't as bad as Galveston. Most of the buildings were standing. I didn't see any bodies lying in the streets. Everybody was in the same shape as me, but some had money. The ones that had money still liked pretty girls. I didn't have to leave town.

I think Faye was worried she might have shocked me with that last statement, because she paused with the telling. I softly whispered, "Please, Faye, go on." Faye raised her chin high and got a triumphant look on her face.

People can say what they want about the way I lived, back then. After the earthquake, I never went hungry, and I never had to sleep outside in a goddamned tent. That's more than I can say for most of the people in the city after the earthquake.

But things didn't stay in a bad way for very long. San Francisco was the most important city on the West Coast back then. Money poured in, and, you know, Tommy, where there's lots of money, there's men who want to spend it. I had a series of rich boyfriends. Married men. They took care of me quite well. I lived in fine apartments and wore nice clothes. I ate in the best restaurants.

Faye paused and slumped her shoulders forward. She closed her eyes. Faye was tired. This was more than she had talked in a long time. Faye jerked her head up with a start. Like she was waking up. I didn't say a word. I didn't want to spoil the moment. I wanted to hear the rest of Faye's story. Fast-forward from the devastating San Francisco earthquake of 1906.

It was 1925. I was thirty-six. That doesn't sound old, but I had a lot of hard miles on me. I'd been around the block lots of times. In any case, I was far too old to play the sweet young thing. They say all the world loves a pretty girl. But they never mention the second part of that saying: There's always a younger pretty girl comin' down the pike. That's a razor that cuts two ways, eh Tommy? I wasn't attracting the same caliber of men. The real high rollers weren't interested in me anymore. I was raised in the life. I knew where that was leading. It's a downhill slide, once you start losing your looks. You know a girl's face is the first thing to go, don't you, Tommy?

I didn't want to end up like my mother, washing other people's shitty drawers. I knew I had to be smarter than my mother. Find me a rich man. Maybe not Nelson Rockefeller, but someone who was doing all right. Someone who could take care of me. Not hit me. Not be too weird in bed. I could even act like I liked the guy. That last part wasn't tough for me. I usually ended up liking my rich boyfriends. It's the way I am.

I went out to hook a sucker but caught a real nice guy. Somebody who deserved a lot better than me.

Faye began to sob. I stood up, walked to the other side of the table, leaned over, and hugged Faye. Now I was crying too. It was a real boo-hoo fest. Faye patted my arm and made a request, "Be a Lovey. Please refresh my drink."

I quickly accomplished that task, but with more flat soda than cheap whiskey. I had been mixing drinks for years. Harsh experience allowed me to discern when someone had enough to drink.

I sat the glass in front of Faye. She thanked me and said, "Have you heard enough for one evening, Tommy?"

I said, "No, I want to hear the story—the whole story. All of it."

Faye gave her head an almost imperceptible nod and began anew.

13

GOLD DUST DREAMS AND HOOKER'S SCHEMES

"Like I said, I just wanted a nice guy who was rich," Faye said, "but I met Carl Wolfe, the best man who was ever born. The love of my life."

A note of recognition chimed in my head when Faye dropped Carl Wolfe's name into the conversation. Faye occasionally mentioned him but always grew sad afterward. I never pressed Faye with questions about Carl. I thought I was finally going to hear about this guy. I wondered what he did to make her feel so bad.

Faye got a serious expression on her face and asked, "Have you ever heard of Frank Delos Wolfe?"

"No."

Faye shook her head in a sad way. "Ah, how quickly the world forgets. Frank Wolfe was one of the most famous architects of his era. He owned three successful architectural firms. Frank Wolfe had a son named Carl. Carl became an architect too. A great one. Better than his father. Carl worked with his father. Sadly, there were far more unhappy times in that collaboration than there were happy ones. Carl and his father quarreled constantly. Their disagreements frequently evolved into great, roaring arguments."

"What did they argue about?"

"About money. There never seemed to be enough. They argued about Carl's fast life. Frank Wolfe believed his son was behaving like a rake."

"Oh."

Faye nodded her head. "But those were the easy arguments, Tommy. It got worse from there. Frank Wolfe invented the California Prairie style of home. Those houses made him rich and famous. He didn't want to venture far from that base. Carl wanted to move forward, venture over new architectural horizons. Carl told Frank Wolfe, 'The California Prairie is yesterday's home. We have built the best of that style already. I am tired of building such things. The buying public is tired of it too.'"

Faye went on. "Frank Wolfe said, 'That's pure hogwash. People like the California Prairie style. You'd better remember which side your bread is buttered on.'"

According to Faye, Carl tried another tack. "He told his father, 'People from all over are coming to California. Some of them are getting away from terrible weather. But do you know what, Dad? Lots of people also come here to escape from boring mid-America.' Carl picked up a magazine. He opened the cover and pointed to a page and said, 'Look. This thing is filled with images of California. Most of them contain Spanish-style buildings, cactus plants, and orange trees. That's what people want to own, a piece of the California dream. They want to live in the land of eternal spring, in Spanish-style houses.'"

The two-way argument continued, as Faye related it.

Frank Wolfe said, "That's pure hogwash. The trash in that magazine is being promoted by hucksters, travel agents, men who tie oranges to scrub brush to convince suckers they are buying orchard homes."

Carl said, "No, that's not it. People who move to San Jose want to buy homes that reflect the unique style of California and the American Southwest."

Frank Wolfe shouted out, "People don't want to live in damned mud brick houses!"

"You're right," Carl told his dad. "I'm not going to build them out of mud bricks. They will be modern houses, with all the conveniences home buyers expect. But when you look at my homes, you will not see much Anglo influence. They will look like old Spain."

Frank Wolfe stormed out of the room. He stopped at the doorway, turned, and spoke. "Build the damned houses that people are used to seeing! That's what turns a profit!"

But do you know what bothered Carl most of all, Tommy? Frank took credit for Carl's work. Said it was his own. Most of the great work that was done by Frank Wolfe's companies after 1912 was done by Carl.

He worked on the California Women's Club. That was the most famous local project of its era. Something interesting happened while they were constructing that building. One of Carl's workmen was digging a trench. He discovered a rough, unglazed, terra-cotta pitcher buried in the dirt. The interior was coated with gold dust. Look over there.

Faye pointed to the shelves that covered the opposite wall. I got up from the bench and stepped over to the shelves. Faye directed my gaze to the shelf. It was lined with old pottery vessels of every description. Faye said, "On the bottom shelf, far left. That one. There. On the end."

I finally noticed a toady-looking pitcher. It was the ugliest, most primitive vessel on the shelf. I thought that couldn't be it. It looks like a kindergartener's first attempt at pottery making. It looks like a mud pie. The thing was so ugly, I didn't want to touch it. I wrinkled my nose and pointed at the pitcher. I asked, "You don't mean that one, do you?"

"Yes. Pick it up. Look inside."

I held the lumpy little pitcher in my hands. I looked inside. There was the gold dust. A lot of gold dust. The rough interior of the pitcher was completely coated. I was amazed. This was just like the adventure stories I read! My mind quickly went through about ten possible scenarios for the pitcher's attribution and its unique coating.

Faye laughed when she saw my reaction to the pitcher. She said, "I can see the wheels going round and round inside your head."

I laughed too. I was a little embarrassed. Faye had caught me daydreaming. I did that a lot.

Faye savored our little moment, then got a wistful expression on her face and said, "Ah, if we had the gold that was once in that pitcher, you and I would have a grand time." Faye looked me in the eye when she voiced those words. I could tell she spoke truly.

I replaced the pitcher on the shelf and sat on the bench. Faye continued.

Carl rebuilt the Rosicrucian complex in San Jose. There was a small reflecting pool on the property. The pool was filled with weeds and mud. Egyptian plants, papyrus and water lilies. The pool had been forgotten by the Rosicrucian staff. It was located right in the middle of where Carl was going to build a new structure. Carl was standing nearby when the workmen drained the pool. He was looking at plans.

The workmen suddenly began to hoot and shout at each other. They were splashing around in the pool. Carl ran over to see what was happening. One of the men reached into the mud and pulled out a huge rainbow trout, it was over three feet long. Carl loved rainbow trout. They were holy things to him. He hated to kill that trout. He wished he could have left it alone, in its own little world.

Those were the days.

Frank Wolfe didn't give Carl credit for anything. Frank Wolfe never made his son a full partner. Carl accumulated a huge load of bitterness.

But I was the fly in the ointment. I was the straw that broke the camel's back. I drove the final wedge between Carl and Frank Wolfe. I'll never forget what happened when Carl took me home to meet Papa.

We drove down the El Camino Real from San Francisco in a fancy car, a Stutz Bearcat roadster. It was fast. It could do a hundred miles an hour. That was a lot in those days. It was foggy when we left the city but cleared up once we got through Redwood City. Carl pulled to the side of the road. He got out and lowered the top. I didn't want him to do that, I was cold. I told Carl, "Don't do that, honey, you're gonna mess up my hair. I want to look nice when I meet your daddy."

Carl laughed and said, "Don't worry, honey, you're gonna knock him off his feet."

I sulked a little bit, but my mood didn't last long. The blue sky and clouds were like the most beautiful ceiling I had ever seen. Besides, it was impossible for me to stay angry very long when I was with Carl. We drove through miles of lovely farmland. Orchards were everywhere. The bay was on one side, the hills on the other. I thought it was the most beautiful place on earth.

We went through about a million little towns. Each one had its own pint-sized downtown. Cars jammed the roads. There seemed to be a lot of traffic for such small places. I asked Carl, "When are we going to get to Willow Glen? And can we put the top up? I'm a city girl. I don't like all this fresh air and wide-open spaces."

Carl just laughed and said, "Faye, I'm an outdoorsman. I like to be outside. If you want to keep up with me, you'd better be outside too."

Then Carl leaned over the seat and kissed me. Not passionately. Sweetly. I knew at that moment I would do anything for Carl Wolfe. If he wanted an outdoorsy-type girl, that's what I would become. Carl drove on. We passed by the most beautiful homes I had ever seen.

Carl said, "This is the Alameda, honey, we're almost there."

Carl turned down a side street. Pretty soon, he stopped the car and said, "Well, honey, this is it—Wolfe Avenue."

I laughed and told Carl, yeah, right, and I'm Leonardo da Vinci. But Carl pointed up at a sign. He said, "No, look, right there. It says Wolfe Avenue."

You know, Tommy, I suppose a normal girl would have been impressed by seeing a street that's named after her fiancé's daddy. But I had met lots of other fathers in lots of other places. I knew that when they owned big chunks of those places, they weren't usually the sort who liked girls like me.

Besides, Tommy, I had already heard plenty about ol' Frank Wolfe, and not just from Carl either. People I knew said he was a tough cookie, real straitlaced. Carl sensed my mood and told me it would be all right. Carl drove a short distance, pointed, and said, "That is the Wolfe mansion."

Tommy, I got scared when I looked up at that giant house. It was creepy looking.

I knew that Carl and I had a great thing going, but I had a bad feeling about this. Carl parked the car and came around and tried to get me out. It took some persuading on his part, I'll tell you. He almost had to drag me. I didn't want to go inside that house. Carl finally succeeded.

He led me up the walkway, pulling me all the way. I was shaking like a leaf. Carl knocked on the door. We waited on the porch for the longest time. I turned around and looked behind me. The place was beautiful. Plants and trees were everywhere. Birds were singing. I could see beautiful homes in the distance. I heard the door open behind me and turned around. An older man was standing in the door. He looked severe, like a Baptist preacher. He didn't seem pleased to see Carl—or me. I thought, so this is the famous Frank Wolfe.

Frank Wolfe said, "Good afternoon, Carl." Then he turned toward me, stuck his chin in the air, looked down his nose, and sneered, "And you would be Miss Faye, I presume?"

Tommy, I lost my voice. I was scared. I stammered out, "Ye-yes—I'm Faye." I stepped up to the door and grabbed his hand and shook it—hard. I damned near did a curtsy. And you know what? That damned Frank Wolfe pulled his hand away from mine. He stepped back, almost stumbled and fell, like he was afraid I had a disease or something. Frank drew in a big breath. I thought he was gonna explode.

He glared at Carl and said, "How dare you bring this, this...prostitute to my front door? I have standing in the community! My reputation has already been damaged by your rakish behavior and profligate ways. But for you to stoop to this level is unconscionable. It is unacceptable!"

At first, Carl behaved like a contrite schoolboy, trying to explain a broken window. He tried to reason with Frank, but got batted down at every turn. Carl was a patient man, but he had his limits. It didn't take Carl long to lose his temper. He blurted out, "Faye is pregnant. She's going to bear your grandchild. I'm going to marry her, with or without your approval."

Frank Wolfe raised himself higher and screamed, "I will not accept a whore for a daughter-in-law."

Tommy, I have been in the middle of a lot of bar fights. I knew where this was going. As soon as Frank Wolfe yelled at Carl, I jumped in between them. That was a good thing, too, because Carl was getting ready to deck his father. I grabbed Carl's arms and screamed, "Don't do it. I'm the problem here. Let me leave. I'll find my own way back home."

I heard Frank Wolfe's voice behind me, saying, "She's right, Carl. She's the problem. Let her leave. For god's sake, man. It's time to grow up. Stop playing with tarts."

I could tell Carl was getting ready to say something else, but Frank Wolfe yelled, "Maybe then I'll make you an equal partner."

Frank Wolfe slammed the door in our faces.

Carl pulled away from me and started yelling at the trees. He turned around, looked at me, and said, "He's never going to let me grow up. In his mind, I'll always be a child. I'm sick of carrying that old man on my back. I want to make a break. Get away from him and his old ideas."

Now, Tommy, I was never a J. P. Morgan, but I had been a businesswoman of sorts for over twenty years. I knew Carl Wolfe needed his father's business connections to make a go of it. I also knew the old man Wolfe needed Carl's ideas and hard work to prop him up. I didn't want their partnership to get busted. I needed Frank Wolfe's money to support the baby that was growing in my belly.

I didn't know much about sex, but I knew that unwanted pregnancies caused a lot of problems. I saw it time and again in my family.

Faye continued with her story. "Things worked out the way I figured. Carl and his father hated each other but knew they couldn't make it alone."

I interjected, "But what about your baby?"

Faye winced at the mention of the child. "Ah, yes, our poor little baby girl was born premature. She weighed just over two pounds, lived a few hours, then died. Carl was bereft. He poured himself into his work. He said, 'I'll build my own things, my own way, no matter what my father thinks.'"

Faye leaned toward me and whispered, "And you know what, Tommy? Carl was right. People loved his new architectural style. They named it Spanish Revival. Countless other people used that style in their buildings, but Carl Wolfe was the real pioneer. By then, Carl had moved completely away from the California Prairie style. So did the home-buying public. Lots of people were beginning to agree with Carl, and all of a sudden, most people seemed to believe the California Prairie style looked dated."

Faye got a triumphant look on her face.

That fell right in with Carl's prediction on the subject.

But that damned Frank Wolfe never admitted he was wrong. That didn't matter to us. We were doing well. Commissions were pouring in. Carl was a great architect. He also had a keen eye for marketing. Carl knew that folks wanted to buy a piece of the California myth. He was just the man to sell it to them. He built and rebuilt more authentic Spanish-type buildings than anyone.

Carl used his experience to build old-looking houses with twentieth-century amenities. That was Carl's version of the modern California home.

But other people began to copy Carl's ideas. He was getting lost in the crowd. Carl said, "I need to show everyone else that I'm the best. It will keep me ahead of the pack. Orders for new houses will pour in. We'll do bigger projects. Subdivisions. I can step out of my father's shadow. I won't need his goddamned full partnership. We'll have all the money we need. I'll buy you gold and jewels."

Carl was a very wise man. He told me apprentices build objects that are called masterpieces. They do this to prove they are craftsmen, that they can stand on their own as tradesmen. "I need to do that, Faye," he said.

I told him, "Honey, you haven't been an apprentice for a very long time." But Carl shook his head. "No, you're wrong. When it comes to this new building style, I am an apprentice. I need to learn the best way to make modern buildings that look old."

"But you've been doing that for years."

"Yes, but I want to learn how to do it better," Carl told me. "I'm going to build my masterpiece. I'm going to build a grand Spanish hacienda, an architectural statement. It will display all that I know and will learn about Spanish Revival architecture."

He drew me into his arms and said, "But this project will be different. I'm building it for you. For us. But first, we must find the perfect location for my hacienda. One that will be a pedestal for its grand style."

Faye paused for a moment, "We bought a huge property outside the San Jose city limits. It began at Monterey Highway and ran for almost a mile along Senter Road. It was over a quarter mile wide. Most of the property is covered with a small mountain."

I finally got the point. Faye was talking about this property and all the stuff around it, even the mountain. I said, "I didn't know that!"

Faye nodded her head. "Nobody does. But it's not big a deal, when you think about it. The mountain was almost worthless, back then. Aside from an abandoned gold mine, there was nothing on it except weeds. It was just another barren wrinkle on California's face. The mountain appeared on the original Spanish land grant as Mesa Dolores. That was a bit too ethnic-sounding for us, so we translated the name into its English version: Mount Dolores."

"Why Dolores?"

"Dolores is my stepdaughter, and I don't want to talk about her."

14

OF TILE MOLDS AND STRAWBERRY POTS

"I'll never forget the day we took possession of our new property. We drove the long way, down Senter Road. When we got to the place where our mountain came in sight, Carl stopped the car. We got out and stood on the roadside. Carl hugged me from behind and whispered in my ear, 'This is all yours, Faye, yours. You won't have to play the rolling stone anymore. This is where you will spend the rest of your life.'"

Faye snorted and laughed, "Dear Carl. Dear, dear Carl. You didn't realize your blessing would become a curse."

That statement floored me. I never thought of Faye's house as being a curse. Then again, I wasn't trapped in that cold place twenty-four hours a day either.

We just stood there on the side of the road and talked. Carl pointed and said, "The hacienda will be right up there, on the mountain crest. On a clear day, you will be able to see all the way to San Francisco and Oakland in the north, to Gilroy in the south. But do you know what I like best about our mountain, Faye?"

I shook my head no.

Carl said, "People will see my building up there. My style. My quality. They will finally realize I am the best architect in California." I turned around and hugged Carl, then whispered into his ear, "I already know you're the best."

Carl returned the kiss, then said, "I appreciate that, but do you know why I'm the best?"

"It's because you work harder than anyone else, sweet cheeks," I told him.

Carl said, "Yes, I work hard but it's really something else. I experiment. I'm not afraid to try new materials. Use unconventional methods. Sometimes my ideas work. Sometimes they don't. But I'm not willing to jump out too far with this project. I don't want to make mistakes. That's why I'm not going to build our hacienda just yet. I'm going to experiment with smaller structures, first. Build some prototypes, to see if my ideas work."

"But how are you going to do that?"

"I'm going to design my experimental buildings from the roof down."

"To keep the rain off, right?"

Carl laughed, and then he said, "You're right in one way but wrong in another. When you look at old Spanish buildings, you can't miss the tile roofs. They provide a unique look. But everyone knows that now. Lots of houses are being built with tile roofs. You can buy clay roof tiles at any local building supply company. But those tiles are made by machines. They are uniform in shape, texture, and color. They don't look authentic."

"Why does that matter?" I asked him.

He said, "The old builders didn't have machines that spit out roof tiles. They made their own, by hand. I have seen lots of roof tiles that date from the Spanish Colonial era. They are rougher in shape and form than modern ones. They aren't all the same color. Some are darker and scorched looking. That's the look I want on my hacienda. I want to make the building look old."

"Why don't you just buy used roof tiles. You know, ones that have been removed from old roofs. You do that, sometimes."

"You're right, Faye,'" he told me, "but salvage tiles always were few and far between. Anyway, the supply dried up years ago."

"Why don't you just buy new handmade roof tiles?"

"Because no one is making them anymore."

Carl was stuck. He didn't want to use new roof tiles on his hacienda. It would look new, another big, overblown, house—just like the ones everybody else was building.

This is where Carl revealed his true genius. He decided to make his own roof tiles, the old Spanish way. But he was smart. Carl didn't want to reinvent a process that had taken thousands of years to develop. He knew he needed help.

Carl said, "I need to find someone who knows the fine details of the tile-making process. But I know that no one in the San Jose area is making tiles by hand. That tradition died out around here seventy years ago."

Carl Wolfe knew lots of people. He asked around. Someone told him that Pima Indians still made handmade roof tiles the old Spanish way. Carl told me, "We have to go to Arizona right now, honey. We will find our tilemakers there."

Tommy, it was the trip of a lifetime. We took the train to Arizona, then hired a car and driver. We drove to lots of Pima Indian villages. Carl asked everyone he met, does anyone around here still make roof tiles by hand? Everyone looked at him like he was crazy. The Indians told Carl, no one does it that way anymore. If you want roof tiles, go back to town and buy them at the hardware store. They've got lots of 'em in there.

But Carl was a determined man. He wasn't ready to give up. We drove all over that damned desert. I must have seen every dried-up, shithole collection of houses in the Southwest. Those people were poor. I was getting ready to jump out of the car and walk a hundred miles back to the train, just to get this over with. I guess that Carl was tired of it, too, because he sadly told me, "I got a lead on a place just down the road. Just let me try once more, honey, then we'll go home."

We stopped in the middle of a scattered collection of houses. I guess they called it a town, but it was nowhere I'd want to live. We walked into a little store. They sold everything, even tacos. We bought some food and talked to the store owner. Carl asked him if he knew of any old Indian potters, men who still made roof tiles by hand.

By that time, Carl flinched every time he asked the question, because he'd been rebuffed so many times.

The store owner laughed. "What are you, some kinda Hollywood moviemaker? Those guys pass through here sometimes. They raise a lot of hell, drink our booze, chase our women, then leave. We don't need that kind of shit no more."

Carl said, "No, no. I'm not a moviemaker. I'm an architect. A builder. I want to use handmade roof tiles on my homes."

The store owner began to laugh—hard. Tommy, he was crying and slapping his pants. The store owner told Carl, "Then you truly are a crazy-assed white man. I like people like you. Sure, I know a guy who used to make those things. But he's kinda old. I don't think he wants to work that hard anymore."

Carl didn't miss a beat. "I don't want his labor, I want his knowledge. Please introduce me to this man."

The store owner got into our car and told our driver where to go. We drove way down a nameless road, then on another for what seemed to be an eternity. We turned down a worse road and drove a bunch more. The store owner was leading us out into the middle of nowhere. Tommy, I remember thinking, is this Indian gonna take us out somewhere and scalp us, leave our bones to bleach in the sun?

Oh, Tommy, I was quite sheltered for one who had lived so hard.

We eventually got to a collection of homes. It was hidden down in a little valley, next to a stream. This place seemed to be more prosperous. Trees were growing all around. They had a large garden growing off to one side. I saw laundry flapping in the breeze—brightly colored clothes.

When we got closer, a bunch of dogs swarmed the car. They barked and snarled like wolves. I thought they were going to jump into the car and tear us apart. But the store owner yelled at the dogs and beat them back with his arm. It was quite a racket.

People walked out into the road and stared at us. They didn't recognize the car. A little boy ran out to the car and called off the dogs. The store owner got out and said, "Thank you, Eli. I don't ever know if those monsters are going to eat me or not."

I interrupted, "But wait. Eli is the name of the Indian who delivers firewood and mows the lawn for you. I never knew another person with that name. He's not the same person, is he?"

Faye got a twinkle in her eye and said, "Well, now. You're just going to have to wait for the answer to that question, aren't you, Tommy?"

Faye's response put me off a little. I wanted to hear all the details at once.

The store owner motioned for me and Carl to get out of the car. We walked toward the gathered people. The store owner introduced us. Someone said, it's too hot to talk out here. Let's go over to the patio.

Tommy, that was the most pleasing news I had heard all day. It was hot. I just wanted to get out of the sun. I followed the Indians toward one of the houses. We passed through some trees and entered a covered patio. It was made of ocotillo brush. It was much cooler in the shade. One of the Indians pointed to some handmade chairs. I collapsed into mine. I was melting.

A young woman walked into the patio and served cool water. She poured it from a large, round jug that had a long neck.

Carl exclaimed, "My god, that's the most beautiful pottery I have ever seen!" The girl who was holding the jug blushed and said, yes, it is. It was made by my grandfather. The girl paused and pointed across the patio, toward a nondescript man who was sitting off by himself. "Him—that man."

Carl looked at the man and said, "So you are the potter I have heard rumors about."

The old potter said, "Yes. I made that jug. I poured my soul into the clay. But I don't do that anymore. The clay took my hands."

The old potter raised his hands into the air. His fingers were twisted and bent. "See my claws. They cannot work anymore. They would just scratch the clay."

The sight of the old potter's useless hands did not deter Carl. He said, "But your mind is quick. I can tell. And you still love clay. I can see it in your eyes. What if we found someone else to be your hands? You can guide them through the process."

The potter said, "No, I am tired. I want to be inside, where it is cool. Not out in the sun, in the clay pits."

Carl said, "That's too bad. I was going to pay you handsomely for your knowledge. But I guess your family is doing so well, they don't need the money."

Tommy, I knew Carl Wolfe better than anybody. I could tell he was so disappointed, he was about ready to cry. But he wasn't about to reveal that fact to the Indians. Carl stood up and thanked the potter for his hospitality. We were almost back to the car when the potter's son called out, "Hey! Did you mean what you said back there? I mean, would you really pay well for what my father knows? Even if he didn't do the labor, himself?"

"Yes, I would pay very well for his knowledge."

The potter's son said, "My father taught me a little bit about pottery. I dug, cleaned, mixed, and pounded the clay. I collected wood and stoked the kilns when the pieces were fired."

The potter's son pointed to the girl who had served the water and said, "My daughter knows about pottery making too."

The granddaughter nodded her head and said, "Yes, I like the clay. I like to hold it in my hands. It feels alive, like I can make anything from it. Maybe even some roof tiles."

The potter's son said, "Thank you, daughter." He turned to Carl and spoke in a serious tone. "We are not so rich that we can walk away from this opportunity. We are doing well, but I see no future for my children here, not all of them, anyway. This may provide a way out for some of them. But there is something else here too. My family worked clay long before white men came, since the beginning of time. My father is the last person to possess the old knowledge about clay. I'd like for someone to pass it on to future generations."

He turned and pointed. "We can rebuild the old kilns— over there. Do you see? We can make you all the tiles you want. Put 'em on a truck or on the train, send 'em straight to you in California."

But that's not what Carl wanted to hear. He told the potter's son, "But I want to make my tiles on the building site. I want to use local materials. That's the way the old ones did it. I also want to learn how to make tiles myself."

Carl's statement upset the potter's son. He got a sour look on his face and said, "I've never been more than fifty miles from this place. I don't want to move my family a thousand miles to make a few roof tiles for a crazy white man."

Tommy, some men might have been upset by having strangers call him crazy. Not Carl Wolfe. His father, everyone else, had been telling Carl his ideas were crazy for years.

Faye got quiet for a moment, stared down into her drink and took a sip. She set the tumbler down and said, "Now look who's crazy. Half the houses in California are built in Carl's style."

I saw the conversation was lagging. I didn't want Faye to stop. I asked, "So did the Indians come to California? Did they make Carl's roof tiles?"

That question snapped Faye out of her funk. "Yes. But only because Carl knew how to deal with reluctant workmen. He told the potter's son, 'I always need workers. You can build the whole house, not just the roof.' That clinched the deal. The Indians accepted Carl's offer. Work was scarce in Arizona. So the Indians came to San Jose. We found places for them to live near Mount Dolores."

Faye got quiet for a moment. To me, it seemed as if she was turning a page in a book and beginning a new chapter. She took a drink and said, "Getting the Indians here turned out to be the easy part. Making clay roof tiles by hand is tricky. It is an exacting, difficult process. That was the hard part."

I interjected, "But all you have to do is slap some clay around and bake it in an oven. We did that in kindergarten."

Faye shot me an intense look and said, "Oh, no, no, no, Tommy. It's not as easy as it looks. Tile roofs are like jigsaw puzzles. The individual pieces must fit perfectly. The roof will leak if the pieces don't match up right." Faye laughed and said, "Carl was a great architect. He never lost sight of a roof's main purpose—to keep the rain off your head."

Faye and I shared a little chuckle over that line. "The Indians told Carl the main trick about making roof tiles. You need to have a good mold."

Faye looked at me and said, "San Jose was the clay tile capital of the world at that time. Carl could have gone to any brickyard in town and bought a hundred molds, a thousand molds, if he wanted. But the tiles that came out of those molds would have been identical to each other. Like they were made by a machine. That would have killed the authentic look Carl wanted."

I asked, "So where did he get his tile molds?"

Faye smiled. "He made them. In the ancient way. Carl sent the old potter and his son out with a pickup truck, a wheelbarrow, and shovel. Carl told the potter's son, 'Take your father up and down Coyote Creek. There are clay deposits all over. Take samples of the clay he likes. Bring 'em back. We'll see which works best. Then we'll know where to get the clay for the hacienda roof.'

"Tommy, the old potter came back with a truckload of wonderful clay. He said it was the best he had ever seen. The potter's son unloaded the clay. He followed his father's preparation directions. The old potter knew all the tricks. Once the clay was ready, the old potter lined up all of Carl's Indian and Mexican workers. He told them, 'Take off your pants. I want to see your legs.'"

I interrupted Faye, "Why did he do that? Did he like boys?"

Faye got a shocked expression on her face and asked, "And how would you know about such things, young man? Hmm."

I blushed and said nothing.

Faye composed herself and continued.

No, Tommy, the old potter didn't like boys. He wanted to judge the size and shape of the men's thighs. He picked three or four individuals he believed had the best-shaped thighs. He told the first man to lie on the ground.

The old potter told his son what to do next: "Place the wet clay on his thigh. From kneecap to crotch. Halfway down his leg on both sides. No more, no less."

The potter's son applied the clay. His father stood by, offering advice when it was needed.

The old potter said, "You must work the clay quickly! Form it into a perfect shape. Smooth out the high and low spots. The water must flow away easily from these tiles. Smooth out the rough edges too. The people will be installing these tiles. We do not want them to cut their hands. But work well, because the shape you make with your hands will remain forever in the mold. Once it is dry, it cannot be changed. The finished tiles will display your mistakes for all to see—forever."

The old potter had sharp words for the men who were lying on the ground: "Be still, twitching lizard, so your movement does not bend the clay!"

The Indians laid on the ground for about an hour. Then came the hard part. The potter's son had to pry the moist clay off the Indians' thighs without causing it to deform. Sometimes they accomplished that. Sometimes they didn't. Lots of the pieces broke when they were lifted away. I came to understand a lot of Indian cuss words that day.

They treated the surviving pieces like holy things. The potter's son gently carried them to an open shed. It was a shady place.

The old potter said, "The clay must dry slowly. Many days. The pieces will explode in the kiln if they dry incompletely or too quickly."

While they were waiting for the clay to dry, they built a kiln, out there in the back.

"You probably noted its remains on your way to the woodshed, Tommy."
I said, "You mean that half-filled hole in the hillside?"
Faye nodded her head.
I said, "Wow! I thought it was just an old trash incinerator."

Well, yes, that's what it is now. But it used to be a large kiln. Carl and his Indians built it from rock they quarried from our mountain. The Indians collected firewood, a lot of firewood. They preferred madrone. They said it would burn longer than oak. It produced a more controllable flame, didn't pop and explode in the kiln.

When the raw tiles were thoroughly dry, men placed them in the kiln. They fired the kiln in the morning. The fire needed constant attention. It burned all day and through the night. The stokers drank homemade mescal. Carl and I stayed with them for a while. One of the Mexicans broke out a guitar. We laughed and sang. Some of the Indians danced. But not like white people; they danced alone. Slowly, with their eyes closed. They held their arms away from their bodies like bird wings, swaying back and forth, like they were in a trance, in another world.

It was such a grand time.

Carl and I went home at midnight. It had been a long day. I slept in late. That habit was a carry-over from the old days, when I stayed up all night at parties. Carl was gone before I got up, but I knew where he was. He came back here to Mount Dolores to see how the firing went.

Later on, Carl told me he was afraid as he drove to the worksite. He knew there were more ways for the firing process to go wrong than right. If just three or four tiles exploded in the kiln, the whole load would be ruined.

Carl pulled onto the road that runs up Mount Dolores. He got out of the car and walked toward the kiln. The place was almost deserted. Most of the crew went home or to other jobs. The old potter was sitting on a stool in front of the kiln. He rose as Carl approached and said, "It's still too hot to touch. But I looked in. From what I can see, it's not too bad. Not many tiles exploded."

Carl was elated. He knew he had made his first mold prototypes. Carl told the old potter, "Even if these molds aren't good, I know how to make them. We can make more."

It took lots of trial and error, but Carl and his Indians eventually got it right. In no time at all, they had a thigh-shaped production mold that was just right. The tiles it made fit perfectly. There were no flaws. But Carl Wolfe was a careful man. He didn't want to commit to a single mold until he had successfully used its product on a building, to make sure the tiles fit and didn't leak. Carl didn't want to run the risk of ruining a large project with his prototype tiles, so he built two small ones.

The gate towers that flank the mountain road behind me. Those are the first prototypes for Carl's new roof style.

I said, "And I thought those things were just pretty little doo-dads. But they're not, they are like the things I build out of my erector set. They are just practice!"

Faye laughed and said, "Oh, Tommy. You are like Carl in so many ways."

I didn't know exactly how to respond to that statement, so I murmured, "Thank you."

Faye nodded her head. "After the towers were complete, Carl sent men up on fruit ladders with buckets of water. They doused the gate tower roofs from every angle. Carl was waiting down below, to see if the roofs leaked. They didn't. Carl gave a loud cheer. His workers joined in. They knew the prototype mold made wonderful tiles."

Closeup of the gate tower roof. These tiles were installed almost 100 years ago. They survived several moderate earthquakes and a huge one. This roof has received very little maintenance. Note that the cement grout is tight around most of the tiles. The tiles have not degenerated. The stucco on the tower walls is thick and rock-hard. The thousand-year-old clear redwood lumber is dried out, but strong. Carl Wolfe built for the ages.

◇◇◇

The remaining Carl Wolfe gate tower. April 2019.

Carl directed his workers to begin producing tiles in quantity. They built a larger kiln. They had many failures, but they needed lots of tiles. The tiles were the main focal point for Carl's unique prototype buildings. Once he had plenty available, he began to think about what he was going to build next.

Many people urged Carl to begin his grand hacienda. But he still wasn't sure about some of the architectural details. Carl's experiments were not complete. He wanted to learn more. Carl decided to build a final prototype, to put all the new details together in one building, to make sure they worked.

And this is where Carl truly displayed his genius and thrift. You see, the prototype guard towers were designed to support a pair of gates. The gates were supposed to control access to the mountain road. Such things are commonly used in Spain and Morocco. Those are tough places. Big gates are heavy. It takes a strong man to open, close, and bar them—a gatekeeper. Gatekeepers need to be on site twenty-four hours a day, to be instantly available when somebody wants to pass through. Old-time Spanish gatekeepers lived in a cottage next to their gates. They were called gatekeeper's cottages.

I was puzzled. I wondered where this rambling story was headed. I opened my mouth to ask a question, but Faye shushed me and said, "Carl Wolfe's final prototype was a gatekeeper's cottage." Faye paused a moment and said, "This cottage."
I said, "Oh."

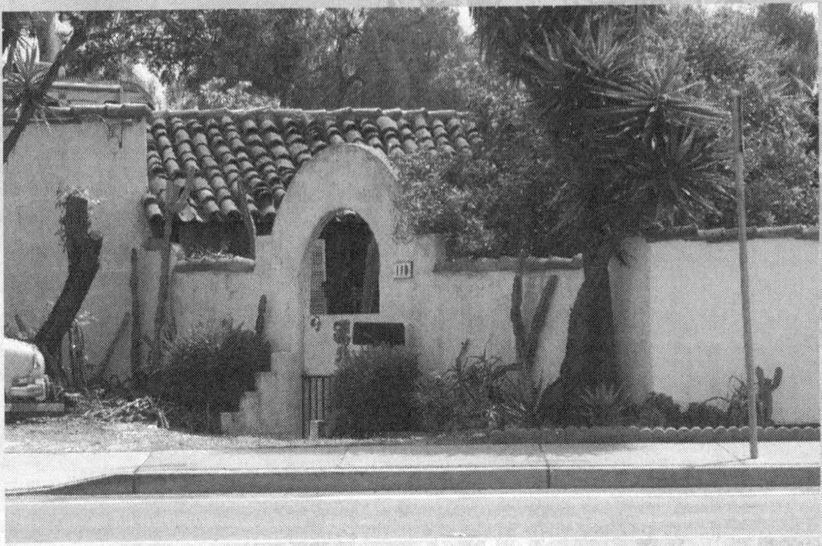

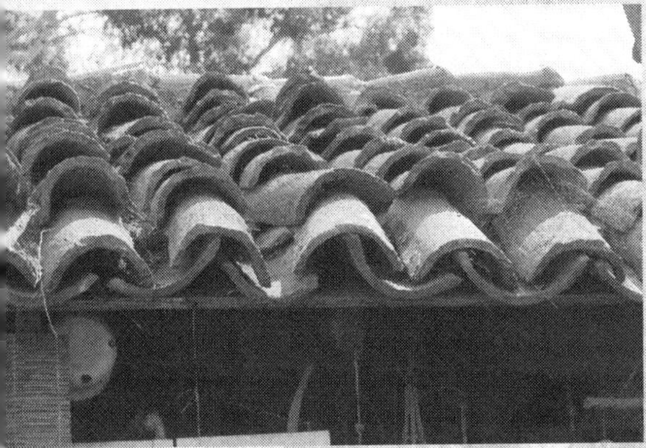

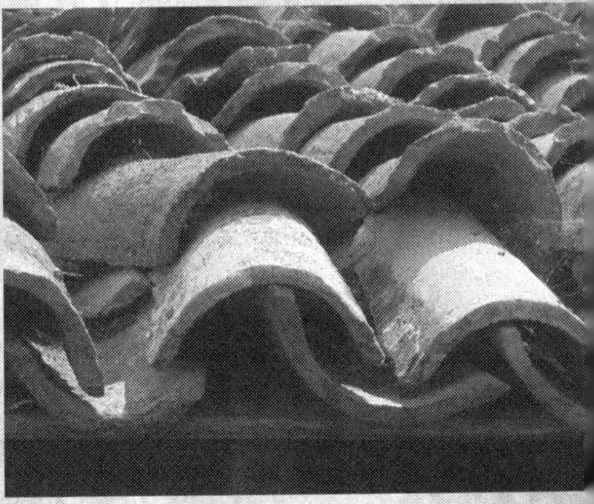

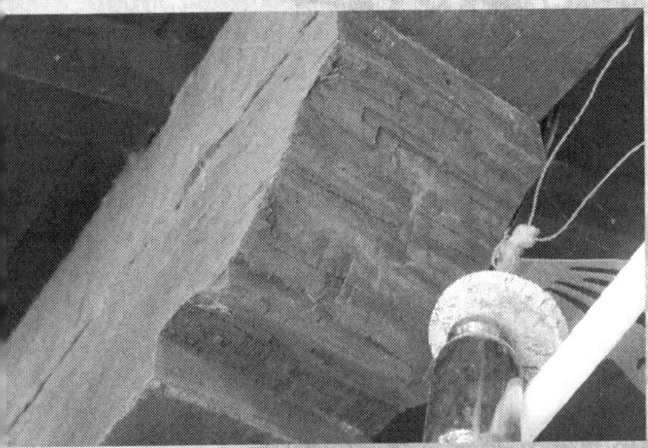

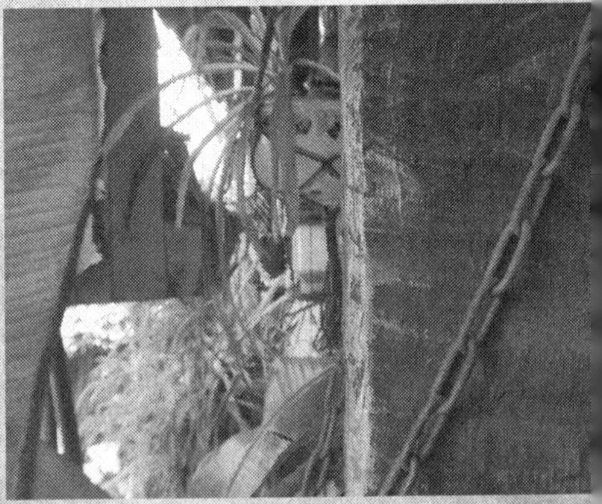

Carl Wolfe's prototype number two: the gatekeeper's cottage, as seen in its present-day, heavily modified condition. A magnificent couple has owned this cottage for almost forty years since Faye's death. They have done a great job of maintaining this property.

◇◇◇

Handmade roof tiles on the Carl Wolfe–designed gatekeeper's cottage. April 2019.

◇◇◇

View of support timbers on the gatekeeper's cottage. California was producing the finest lumber in the world during Carl Wolfe's era. He could have walked into a hundred lumberyards and bought wonderful, finished beams. But those beams would have been smooth and new-looking. Carl wanted his structures to look old. A long-dead and forgotten tradesman shaped this roof beam support block using a crosscut saw, adze, mallet, and chisel. Note the tool marks in the ancient redwood.

◇◇◇

Adze marks on a porch support post at the Wolfe gatekeeper's cottage. These beams looked old the day they were installed, yet they are still strong, almost 100 years later.

Faye stopped talking. I didn't know what to say. You could have heard a pin drop in that room. I finally came up with a boy-like question: "Did you really have a gatekeeper, Faye?"

She laughed and said, "No. We never installed any gates. The guard towers and gatekeeper's cottage were focal points. They were meant to serve just one purpose—grab people's attention as they drove down Senter Road. Carl said they were like billboards, but prettier."

Faye laughed at Carl's joke. No one had heard that punch line in more than thirty years. The humor seemed to renew her energy. It had been a long night.

15

THE GATEKEEPER'S COTTAGE

"Carl Wolfe was too frugal to build a home that was only good for advertising purposes," Faye said. "It also had to be useful for something else. Carl used the gatekeeper's cottage to conduct more experiments, to pull some final architectural details together. But most of all, Carl intended the gatekeeper's cottage to be a model home. To show people the things they could have, if Carl Wolfe built their home."

I said, "Really? Me 'n Frank and Lita have looked at about a zillion model homes. They were all alike: new, cheap, crappy-looking little boxes. Except for the trim, they all looked alike. I didn't think Carl would build something like that. I thought this house was ancient. From the Spanish era. I would have never guessed it was a model home."

Faye beamed and nodded her head. She said, "Yes! That was the gist of Carl Wolfe's architectural vision. A new house that looks ancient! Carl built his final prototype—this house, I mean. The structure was flawless. Carl built it strong. He knew we have more earthquakes than they do in Spain. But one detail remained incomplete: the roof."

I asked, "Why? Carl already made the tiles."

"You're right, Tommy, but the old potter told us he always put the roof on last. It is traditional. It is their way of blessing the house, or like putting a hat on a beautiful woman before she goes out the door."

I blushed when the old potter said that to me. Carl gave me a big hug.

Anyway, Carl had his own reasons for wanting to put the roof tiles on last. He didn't want them to get chipped or broken while they were doing other things. He didn't want them to get spattered with stucco and paint.

The Indians installed the roof tiles. They fit perfectly. The tiles looked like they were two hundred years old. Carl ran more water tests. The roof didn't leak.

It was the happiest moment of Carl Wolfe's life. The validation of his ideas, his hopes and dreams, for him and me—and the Indians. They risked a lot by coming up here.

[Faye pointed up at the ceiling.] No one ever notices those tiles. If they do, then they think it's just another roof. But I'll tell you what, Tommy, it was a big deal to Carl and his workers when they finished it. It was the end of a unique process that bonded builder and craftsman.

Carl Wolfe threw a Spanish-style fiesta to celebrate his success and to be a housewarming for us. The party was held in the side yard of the gatekeeper's cottage—out beyond the woodshed, under the pepper tree. Carl and I had many friends. They mixed with the workers. It was the hit of the San Jose social season. Our Mexican workers cooked a whole calf and some baby goats. They did it in a hole in the ground. They wrapped the carcasses in agave and banana leaves. The meat was succulent. The workers' wives made tortillas and salsa. We had mescal, music, and dancing.

Later in the evening, the potter's son stood up. He raised his hands and called for silence. The potter's son asked his father to step forward. The potter walked to his son and spoke quietly in his ear. The potter's son said, "Please, father. Say it yourself."

The potter nodded his head and faced me and Carl. The potter began to speak: "I remember the old days. When we built houses with our hands from what came from the earth. Nothing from the store. The people came together and made this happen. When we made the roof tiles, we always had some clay left. More than we needed." The old potter smiled and said, "But that was kind of a planned thing. On purpose. We wanted the extra clay to make a little something, a gift for the wife of the man who built the house."

Tommy, the place was packed, but suddenly, the crowd parted. The potter's granddaughter slowly walked through the crowd. She was carrying something large. Her arms were wrapped around it. She walked toward me and placed the object on the ground.

The potter's granddaughter said, "This is an olla. Anglos call them strawberry pots. Look, it has many cups, so you can plant strawberries. The berries will hang down. You can come out to pick them in the morning, to give to your handsome husband for breakfast." The girl began to blush and stammer. I could tell she was having trouble saying something.

The potter's son said, "Go ahead, daughter, it's okay."

The potter's granddaughter said, "I made this for you, with my grandfather's help. He watched me, told me what to do. It is my first big project." The girl reddened, shed a tear, and said, "He says it was his last."

We both sat quietly. I was thinking about what Faye said. Then I came to a great realization. "Wait a minute, Faye, there is a strawberry pot out on the porch. Is it the same one?"

Faye nodded, "Yes."

I said, "Cool. I love strawberry pots! That's the nicest one I ever saw!"

"Yes, it's the best of its kind. Other people know that too. The potter got famous, after he died. Several museums have asked to acquire it. The strawberry pot is a unique historical artifact. But it is much more than that to me. The strawberry pot reminds me of Carl. It reminds me of the best day of my life."

Faye paused. She gazed over my shoulder, into the distance of a long-forgotten land. She had a wistful look on her face. "We were all so hopeful. Carl, the Indians, and me all believed this was the beginning of a great new thing. Everyone would have jobs. Carl would get the money he needed to build his grand hacienda."

I interjected, "That's neat!"

Faye winced and said, "No. It wasn't."

"Why?"

"Because of the 1929 stock market crash."

I said, "Oh." No one had to explain that event to me. My parents were raised during the Depression that followed the 1929 crash. They had it rough.

Faye nodded her head in agreement. "People stopped buying houses. People stopped building houses. After Frank Wolfe died, Carl finally became a full partner in the family business. But it was too late to help Carl—or me. There wasn't enough work to support us in the style to which we had become accustomed. Carl abandoned his plans to build a grand hacienda. We were just trying to survive. We didn't have enough work to keep the full crew going. Most of the Indians went back to Arizona. Just one of them stayed behind. Eli."

I said, "So Eli is your last Indian!"

"Yes. Eli is the potter's grandson."

I interjected, "But why didn't Eli go back to Arizona with the other Indians?"

"Because Eli's father only wanted him to drink on feast days. Eli wanted to get drunk all the time. They had a great, roiling argument. Eli's father told him, if you stay here, people will see you as a drunken, brown-skinned man. They will think you are just another goddamned wetback Mexican!"

Faye got quiet for a moment. She fidgeted with her glass. "Carl and I encouraged Eli. We wanted him to become a contractor. Eli is a good carpenter when he is sober."

I sneered, "If he ever gets sober."

Faye shot me an angry look and barked, "Don't you dare say that, Tommy! You don't know what Eli has been through. He was in a tank during World War II. That's why he's deaf, the noise from the guns."

"Oh."

Faye was on a roll now. "Yes, and his tank got hit by a German 88-millimeter shell. Eli was covered with his best friend's brains. Eli was wounded too. So you better be nice to him, Tommy!"

I was embarrassed. This was the first time that Faye ever yelled at me. Faye's words stung me to the core. Then there was the other part: I wasn't going to be anything to Eli, nice or otherwise. I was afraid of the mean sonofabitch.

Faye looked at me and said, "I'm sorry, Tommy, but it's a sore subject for me to talk about. I hate to see what Eli has become."

"That's all right, Faye. I was wrong. Eli is my elder. You're always supposed to speak well of your elders."

Faye laughed. "That's a nice idea. I just wish it was always possible."

It got quiet in the room. But Faye still seemed to have a lot of energy, so I asked, "What happened next, I mean, after the stock market crashed?"

Faye said, "We moved into the gatekeeper's cottage. This house."

"Cool! This is where I would have wanted to live too!"

Faye sighed and said, "Ah, Tommy. You have so much to learn about life and living. We didn't want to move in here."

I asked, "But what's so bad about it?"

Faye said, "This house wasn't designed to be inhabited. It is just a test mule, a department store mannequin, a model."

Now it was my turn to be a little outraged, "Yeah, but it has walls, a roof, and a big, soft bed—and that great little stove. It's better than most of the dumps I've lived in."

Faye was taken aback by my words. I could tell she felt humbled. "Yes, Tommy, you are right. We should always be grateful to have a roof over our heads. But this house lacks some essential amenities, like a decent heating system and reliable hot water. This joint is cold as a tomb, most of the time. That detail might not be as important when you're young, but when you're old, it gets in your bones."

I said, "Oh, yeah. I forgot about that. I'm sorry."

Faye nodded her head, "Yes. Carl built the cottage to look like it was built in the eighteenth century. He succeeded with that goal. But it sure makes for tough living in the twentieth century. But Carl and I made do. We had nowhere else to go. But it wasn't the kind of life either of us had ever imagined. I mean, I was born poor, but I had lived high for a long time. And, anyway, I was used to getting pulled down by the Mariah part of my name.

"Poor Carl had a tougher time with it. He had been rich his whole life, the best of everything. Carl had been a big man around town for a long time. He built the prettiest buildings in town. He told everyone about the grand hacienda he was going to build. Then he went begging for second-rate jobs and moved into a third-rate home."

Faye got quiet for a moment. "You know, Tommy, you just don't know how much you can take until you have to."

"What do you mean?"

"I spent my whole life chasing rich men and money. I found my rich man, then he went broke on me. Twenty years before, I might have dumped the guy." Faye clenched her eyes shut, furiously shook her head from side to side, and said, "No, no, no, I wouldn't have left Carl Wolfe. Not ever. He made me laugh. He made me happy. I would have worn rags and followed him into hell, just to be with him."

"But what did you do to make money?"

"Carl still got a few jobs, here and there. It was barely enough to keep the lights on in this place. But it was paid for and the taxes were low, so we just kept going. And you know what, Tommy? We still had a good time. We found other things to do, things that didn't require much money. To be honest about it, we had more fun when we were broke."

I asked, "What do you mean?"

"When Carl was rich and famous, he was busy all the time. He didn't get to do the quiet things he enjoyed, like trout fishing. Carl loved to be in the Santa Cruz Mountains, down some canyon, wading in a stream. He didn't care if he caught anything or not." Faye laughed, "At least that's what he said. But he sure did try hard to catch 'em, and he always did. Carl Wolfe could do just about anything he set his mind to."

I said, "Cool! I love trout fishing, except for the packing and unpacking it takes so that we can camp by the stream."

Faye's gaze took her to a place far away in time and memory.

We were too broke to do it that way. We packed light, just coffee grounds, an old enamel coffeepot, and two raw eggs. We headed off in the wee hours of the morning. By sunup we were in the Santa Cruz Mountains on the banks of the San Lorenzo River. Carl filled the coffeepot with water. Oh, that sweet mountain water. Nothing tastes better. Carl put the pot with the eggs, coffee grounds, and water on the edge of a little campfire.

Carl said, "I'm gonna go catch us a fat trout to go with those eggs. Sit here and watch the fire. Don't let it spread. We don't want to start a forest fire. We already have enough trouble."

I sat. I was freezing my ass off but happy. Carl returned in about an hour. He had two eight-inch rainbow trout cleaned and threaded on green willow sticks. I laughed when I saw those little fish and asked Carl why he didn't throw those poor things back and catch a big one.

Carl said, "I caught two nice steelhead, but put 'em back in the river. I won't kill a big trout. We need 'em to make baby trout. The small ones taste better anyway."

Carl slowly roasted the trout over the coals. It seemed to take forever. The fish were fatter than they looked. The oil dripped onto the coals. Tommy, it smelled better than any smoked salmon.

Carl poured us a cup of coffee. It was too strong and filled with grounds, like drinking birdshot. He fished the eggs out of the pot with a stick. Carl took a twist of salt out of his shirt pocket and sprinkled it on the eggs and fish. It was the best meal of my life.

Faye got quiet, again. I could see she was tired. But I was being selfish. I didn't want her to stop. I sensed we were getting closer to the end of the story.

I quickly asked, "What else did you and Carl do, when you were broke, I mean, besides trout fishing?"

Faye said, "We talked and talked and talked and talked. We never seemed to grow weary of each other's conversation, though Carl Wolfe could be hard to take sometimes. He was a man of strong opinions."

I asked, "How so?"

Like the first night we moved into the cottage. The inside walls were painted pure, blinding white. I loved the color. It looked so fresh and clean.

Carl said, "I'm glad that you like the color of the walls. It mimics the lime whitewash the Spaniards used as paint. But the walls in old-time houses didn't stay white for very long. Smoke from fireplaces and tallow candles quickly stained the whitewash."

Carl dipped a handful of rags in used motor oil. He stood on a ladder and began to rub the oil-soaked rags all over the walls and ceiling. I had a fit when I saw what he was doing. I followed him around the room. I was crying, screaming, begging him to stop marring the paint. I tried to pull him off the ladder, but he wouldn't stop. He just laughed me off and said he was doing the right thing. That really made me mad. We got into a furious argument. The worst we ever had. I stormed out of the house and took a walk up the Mount Dolores road.

Pretty soon, I was more tired than I was mad. I walked back down the hill. I dreaded the thought of what was waiting for me at home. I expected to see the worst kind of gummed-up, oily stains on my pristine new walls. But I caught myself. I thought, hell, Faye. You've been though worse than this with guys. Just go along.

I walked into the house and was amazed at the transformation. Carl had applied the oil in artistic patterns. He put more above and around the huge Spanish fireplace.

In just a few minutes, Carl made the walls and ceiling look like they were two hundred years old. It was the prettiest thing I ever saw.

When Carl heard me open the door, he walked in from the kitchen. He was drying his hands.

"Well, Faye," he said, "what do you think now?"

It was the lowest point of my life. I felt like a first-class shit heel. A few minutes before, I had called Carl every name in the book, not good ones either. But he was right. The walls looked better after he had smeared them with oil.

Faye began to weep. These were the worst tears of the night. She removed her glasses and wiped her eyes. Faye said, "I was such a fool. I would give anything to be able to go back and live that moment differently. I was so hard on Carl sometimes. We were happy together."

I sat there, staring at the table. I eventually broke the silence, "Tell me more about your life with Carl, please."

Faye winced when she heard my request. It touched a nerve, but she answered, anyway. "We planned to see the world, the great architecture of Spain and Italy. Carl was always looking for new design elements. But that didn't happen. We didn't even have money to go up to San Francisco for dinner and dancing. So, we made do, right here."

"How did you do that?"

Faye stared into the distance, lost in thought.

I didn't, Carl did. One day, I was complaining about the house, how it was cold and ugly. Carl took my hand and said, "Come with me. Let's go outside."

Carl led me across Senter Road. We turned and looked back at our home. Carl said, "Faye, do you remember the houses we saw in Arizona?"

I nodded my head. "Yeah, most of 'em were old, squat, and ugly, just like that one." I jabbed my finger at the gatekeeper's cottage for emphasis.

Carl pulled me toward him and gave me a big hug. "Now, Faye. I know this isn't what we had planned, but it's all we have. I agree, the house does look ugly, sitting all by itself on a bare mountainside, stuck between two dirt roads. But we can change that. We can make the place look pretty."

And then I said, "Yeah, but how do you put lipstick on that pig?"

To which Carl said, "We'll plant a garden. Just like the ones we saw in Arizona. The plants will soften the lines and make the house blend into its surroundings."

I wasn't a gardener. That was Carl's thing. But I went along, because I wanted to be with him. I was also bored stiff. I was tired of sitting around all day, filing my nails. The damned things were ground down to the quick.

So we began to collect cactus and other desert plants.

I wrinkled my nose, "Why cactus?"

Faye said, "Because the soil here is thin. It is made from serpentine rock. Not much else will grow."

I said, "Oh, that's too bad." I spent untold hours reading college-level horticultural books, but none of them were about cactus. But I did know about serpentine soils. They are one of the worst types in San Jose.

Faye said, "I know you don't like cactus, but they sure do grow well here, don't they?"

I said, "Oh yes. The plants are beautiful. They look like they are two hundred years old."

Faye nodded her head, "There was another reason we planted cactus; they were free. Cactus multiply. People gave us their extra plants. Carl and I planted cactus everywhere, every kind we could get. Some of them didn't do well, but most thrived. The collection grew and grew.

"But you know, Tommy, sometimes people gave us artifacts to put in the garden, to add a little more spice."

"Artifacts, like what?"

"Like the chopping block you use for my kindling. It was given to Carl by Antonio Andres Bernal. He was the last owner of the Santa Teresa Rancho. People around here called him the last Spanish Don."

I said, "Then I'd better be more careful when I chop on the old block."

"I don't think you have to worry much. That block was solid the last time I saw it. Anyway, Don Bernal said it came from the old rancho, from a giant oak limb that fell off in front of the main house during a big storm. Don Bernal gave that block to Carl so that he would preserve it, but look what's happened now.

A starving kid from nowhere is using it to split junk for an indigent old woman's fire."

That thought seemed to bring Faye down. She got quiet.

I asked, "Have you had enough for one night? I mean, should I go home?"

Faye shook her head in an emphatic way as she said, "No, I have to finish this. Someone—you—needs to hear the truth.

"Carl Wolfe didn't want to spend his days on a scorching hillside, in the garden. He wanted to build houses. I mean, Carl still got a few building jobs, but it was nothing like before. Carl pretended it didn't bother him, but it did."

Faye paused and took a drink. She tilted the glass and looked at the bottom. "People told me that Carl Wolfe was always a flashy dresser, even when he was a child. Later on, he drove nice cars. He didn't like wearing old suits and driving cars with bald tires."

Faye stopped talking. She looked down. Into her glass. Into the dark places of her memory. The seconds ticked by.

Faye finally looked at me. "They say Carl Wolfe died of natural causes. They called it 'an untimely death.' He was just fifty-one. But I know the truth. He killed himself."

16

ONCE A MOUNTAIN, NOW A MOLE HILL

Boom. It felt like a bomb went off in my head. Carl killed himself? Aw hell, Tommy. Why did you press her to talk about this stuff? I felt horrible because I made Faye relive the pain. I began to cry. "I'm sorry, Faye."

Faye started to cry too. "That's a lot for a young man to handle, I know. But it was a lot for me too. Thank god I had an understanding doctor. He wrote the natural causes dodge to help me out."

I asked, "Why?"

"Because the doctor knew Carl had a little insurance policy. It was null and void in case of suicide."

"Oh."

Faye grew quiet for a moment. "I knew that doctor for years, right through the Great Depression. Him and me had drinks, sometimes. The doctor told me he wrote natural causes all the time when it wasn't. He said it was no big deal, just a sign of the times."

Faye looked down. "The shit really hit the fan after Carl died. I spent the preceding years being the wife of the great Carl Wolfe. Even when we were poor, that meant something. Everyone treated me nice. That changed once Carl was gone. In their eyes, I became the aged hooker who snared a rich guy and waited for him to die."

Faye paused. "Lots of people blamed me for the split that happened between father and son. They said I broke up the great Wolfe dynasty." Faye snorted. "There never was a dynasty in that family. Frank Wolfe didn't give Carl the sweat off his balls."

That expression floored me. I'd heard it used many times, but never by a woman.

Faye was pissed. "Some folks thought I shouldn't inherit Mount Dolores. They made noises like they were going to fight me in court and take it away from me. But Carl set things up right, legally. He left everything to me, even his debts. People didn't fight me over those. They were all mine. I had to find a way to make some money. I didn't want to lose this place. It was all that remained of Carl Wolfe, his last great work.

"Tommy, I was in a real pickle. I was fifty years old. I knew I would never attract another man who would take care of me. I knew I was going to have to make it on my own. I got a job working as a school cook. That was rough. The head cook was a tyrant. I worked there because the pay was regular, and I got to eat all I wanted. That last part was important, sometimes."

Faye said, "Learn how to cook in restaurants, Tommy. The pay may not be great, but you won't ever go hungry. You never know when a job benefit like that might come in handy."

I was hungry as hell at that moment, so I had no problem finding an answer. "That sounds like a great idea."

Faye nodded her head and continued, "I eventually got a job as a county social worker. The work was easy on the back, but hard on the soul."

"Why?"

Faye said, "My boss knew I had dealt with Carl's Indian and Mexican workers. I had a little Spanish. The county sent me out to deal with their Mexican cases. I didn't like what I saw. Older men seduced very young women—girls, really—thirteen, fourteen, fifteen years old. They got 'em pregnant right away and tied 'em down with a kid. Then they beat the girls up and left 'em alone. I saw it happen time and again."

I said, "Oh. That's too bad." But I didn't say what I was really thinking: Gee, that's a switch. In my family, the women beat on the men and leave them.

Faye continued. "Some of the women were heroic. They were wonderful mothers, marvelous people." She said, "But most of them were lazy pigs. I remember one in particular. She boiled a huge pot of beans every three or four days. The woman stuck the pot in the middle of the kitchen table. The beans congealed into a gelatinous mass. Her children used their bare hands to scoop the beans into their mouths. You could see the impression of the tiny hands in the rotten, congealed beans. When the pot was empty, the woman boiled another batch of beans in the unwashed pot. It made me cry to see that. I couldn't stand seeing destitute people every day. I quit the social worker job."

"But how did you get by?" I asked Faye. "Where did you get money?"

Faye said, "I sold off pieces of the land Carl and I bought. All of Mount Dolores and the field that runs down to Monterey Highway, where the trailer park is located."

"Wow! That's a lot of land."

Faye said, "Yes, it is. But I didn't get a lot of money for it. Barren mountainsides weren't worth much, back then. But it was enough to pay off Carl's debts and put food on my table."

Faye sighed and said, "Now they're building thousands of new homes up there. What a difference thirty years makes. If I still owned that property, I'd be a millionaire. But that's the Mariah side of my life, ain't it, Tommy?"

I knew it would be polite for me to say something at this point, but couldn't think of much, except, "If it was you selling the house lots, we'd have a grand time, wouldn't we?"

Faye laughed when she heard me use one of her favored expressions. "Yes, we would."

Faye looked at me. "Listen to me whine. I'm making it sound like it was all bad, but it wasn't. There were plenty of good times too. My old friends, the ones I knew before I met Carl, were true to me. They came to see me here. We talked about the old days, when we were young, beautiful, and happy.

"I also made new friends. They didn't care what I used to be. I eventually met a nice man. His name was John. He was a widower. John said he never wanted to get married again. He just wanted to be good friends with me. Oh, Tommy, John and I were friends for a very long time. I lost him not long before you came around."

Faye clenched her eyes tightly closed and said, "I'm not going to cry about this. I must get through the story. I want you to hear it all—before I die."

"No! Don't talk like that!" I stood and yelled at Faye. "You're fine! You can't die! I only had one other friend and he just died. You can't leave me alone!"

I began to weep inconsolably. Faye was crying too. I finally sat down and composed myself. "I'm sorry. I shouldn't have behaved that way. Just tell me your story and don't talk about dying ever again. Please."

Help arrived from an unexpected quarter. The cactus garden thrived. The plants reproduced like crazy. I gave some of them a little help, in that regard. They are so easy to propagate. I had lots of cactus plants. Pretty ones. Rare ones too.

Senter Road gets a lot of traffic. The garden really stood out. People saw the cactus and stopped. They wanted to look around. Lots of them wanted to buy plants. I made good money selling plants. Not enough to live on, but it helped.

That's another thing you ought to learn. How to sell plants. You are a natural plant man, Tommy.

I had a marvelous life. I didn't have much money, but I didn't have a mortgage either. I didn't need much to live. I had lots of visitors, so I wasn't alone.

Things could have gone on like that for a long time. But they didn't. The Mariah part of my name always comes back to haunt me. We didn't have regular trash pickup out here until a few years ago. Some people collected their trash and took it to the dump. Not me. I burned my trash and yard waste in the remains of Carl's old tile kiln. I mean, not the kiln itself. We had to tear that down when we built the house. It was in the way. But part of the old kiln remained, the hollow place in the hillside.

I was burning pepper tree leaves in the hollow. The leaves were damp and small; they clumped together and weren't burning well, just smoldering. I didn't like that. It was cold outside. I wanted to get back inside. It got to a point where the leaves weren't burning at all so I began to vigorously stir the smoldering mass with a rake.

I slipped and fell into the fire pit. I sat right down in the burning leaves. My round bottom fit tightly in the bottom of the fire pit, just like it was an easy chair. I was stuck tight in the middle of the smoldering leaves. I couldn't pull myself up, the fire was three feet wide. Every time I tried to push myself up, I burned my hands. I was screaming my head off. A neighbor heard me and came running down the hill. He saw what was happening and pulled me out of the hole, but I collapsed on the ground. My clothes were on fire. My neighbor took off his jacket and used it to beat out the flames.

I don't remember anything after that. I woke up in the county hospital a few days later. They were keeping me doped up because I was burned so bad. I wish they would have kept me doped up too. It hurt like hell. No, it was worse than hell. You don't want to know. The pain gradually subsided. I healed. I mean, my skin kind of healed. But the muscles on my backside and legs were cooked. The tendons froze up. I could barely move my legs. I became a cripple.

Other people have to do everything for me now. I can't drive my car. It's rotting out in the garage. I can't go out in my garden.

Carl said I would spend the rest of my life here. He meant that as a blessing, but it turned out to be a curse. Carl's house became my prison. And that's where you came in, Tommy.

Faye wanted me to have her car, and we agreed on a price. Before I was able to raise the money, the housekeeper's boyfriend offered Faye a highball price—if Faye agreed to sell it to him on credit. Faye agreed; the man took the car, dumped the girlfriend, and never paid Faye.

Faye was bitterly disappointed and said at the time, "Oh, Lovey, I wanted the money so that you and I could go out and have a grand time together, just once." Faye, my girl, your best intentions always seemed to fall on stony ground. You and I were two of a kind.

Faye held my gaze for a long time. My mind was filled with Faye—and her story.

Faye looked down at her empty glass and said, "Oh, my, where did the evening go? Tommy, would you please stoke the fire for me, one last time? It will be warmer when I go to bed, and I'll have a little hot water too."

I said, "Sure, Faye. I've got to get to bed too. I want to work in my garden tomorrow."

"That will be grand for you."

I stoked the fire and helped Faye get into bed. She said, "This mattress is from the last century, but it's covered with an electric blanket. I think I have the best of both worlds here."

I leaned in to give Faye a hug. She pulled me in hard and gave me a real bear hug. When I finally stood, Faye said, "You are such a lovey to listen to a bunch of dry old stuff that happened a very long time ago. Go out there and be with people your own age."

◇◇◇

Faye Wolfe's 1937 Plymouth coupe, parked in the Carl Wolfe
gatekeeper's cottage garage. Faye stood less than five feet
tall and couldn't reach the control pedals. She directed Eli,
her Indian carpenter, to screw wooden blocks to the pedals.

I shook my head, "No. I don't understand my generation. People my age went crazy when the Beatles arrived. I like Mozart and Richard Strauss and Luther Burbank. My classmates think I'm weird."

Faye said, "All that will change when the girls discover what a lovey you are. Now go home. Leave a lady to her toilet."

I walked out the side door. Faye's cat, Missy, was waiting patiently. I reopened the door and let the cat into the cottage. I watched her as she passed. I remember thinking, yes, Missy, you do have pantaloons, just like Faye says.

17

CLEOPATRA AND MAX

I stood on Faye's side porch for a long while. The lights of San Jose were just a faint glow in the northern sky. But that light was enough to reveal the silhouettes of the tall cactus plants that stood in front of me. There must have been a moon out, too, because the sandy beds were glowing, just a little. I could see the faint outlines of the winding pathways that curled around the garden.

I walked away from Faye's door and stepped out on the gravel road. I thought, Carl Wolfe's road. I know that now. I paused and looked down the hill, toward the trailer park. The lights were off in Max Gosseling's trailer. He must be at the movies.

Then I remembered something: I had to do a big job for Max tomorrow. I couldn't work in my garden. But I wasn't disappointed. Frank and Lita were in Reno. I knew they would be gone for two more days. They didn't have much time to do grocery shopping before they left. Our kitchen cupboards were almost empty. The money I made working for Max would buy me a cheeseburger and fries. I was happy.

I looked east and west down Senter Road before I emerged from the tamarisk bushes that stood in front of Faye's property. People drove fast along that stretch. I didn't want to get run over.

But I was really watching for worse things than speeding cars. It was less than a quarter mile from Faye's house to mine, but it seemed more like a thousand. Our neighborhood was rough and getting rougher. It was bad enough during the day, but horrid at night. Mexican gang members roamed in packs. The most dangerous predators preferred to hunt alone. I jumped on my bicycle and pedaled like crazy.

My cat, Puff, was sitting on our front doorstep. He was my best friend at home. I entered the house and heard my other best friend scratching on the patio door. He was a marvelous little Labrador retriever mix named Black.

Black was a real toughie; he was the only creature I ever met who was able to make Frank McMillan back down. That happened when Frank came in my room to engage in some of his usual nighttime Tommy-knocking. Black ferociously tore into Frank and nipped him several times. The little dog never slept indoors again.

I pray there is a heaven, so I can revisit the angels god sent to me. I pray there is a hell so Frank will be there.

I gave both animals love and bowls of food. I made an egg sandwich for myself. I took a bath and went to bed. I was happy. I knew Frank McMillan was 250 miles away. I didn't have to wonder if he would pound me against the wall in the middle of the night. I fell into a deep sleep.

Morning dawned bright and clear. I quickly fed myself and the animals. I was in a hurry; Max wanted to get started at eight. I rode my bike to Max's trailer and parked it under the front awning. The awning I had installed. I had drilled the holes for the lead anchors with a hand auger and five-pound sledgehammer. I did a good job. They held tight through the last storm. I looked forward

◇◇◇

This picture contains the most important elements of my
home life at age fifteen: music, gardening, and my dog, Black.

and thought about how I had blocked and leveled Max's new fifty-five-foot-long trailer too. I was just fifteen, but I took great pride in doing a job well.

I didn't bother to knock on Max's front door; I walked right through. I was now a longtime employee. Max trusted me completely. He was washing his breakfast dishes as I entered. Max turned away from the sink and said, "Look at you, kid. You look worn out. I'll bet you were chasing girls all night. Give the girls a rest. Get more sleep, then you'll be worth something to me on Saturday morning."

Anyone who overheard Max's words might have thought he was being mean. He wasn't. He was teasing me, reminding me about what was important in life, at work and away.

Max said, "Well, kid, I ain't got all day. The letterpress is inked up. I did the job before you got here. Clean it."

I had been cleaning Max's letterpresses for about four years. We were like an old married couple. We'd finish each other's sentences. As soon as Max said, "Clean it," I began to repeat his standard second line, "Clean enough to use white or yellow ink." White and yellow ink required a very clean press. Max Gosseling used a lot of yellow ink. Black ink too. Max's ink choices bought me a lot of cheeseburgers.

I cleaned the letterpress and broke down the type. Each piece went into its private cubbyhole. There were about 10,000 cubbyholes in Max's type cases. There was no room for error. Max had only a few pieces of certain type; they had to be in the right places when he went to find them, next time.

Max Gosseling didn't always have work for me to do. Because of that lack, I never stopped looking for other jobs, especially those that involved gardening and weeding. Competition was fierce for that work in our neighborhood. I didn't get a lot of jobs, no matter how hard I tried. Max thought I just needed to do a little advertising, but said, "I'm too busy to do it for ya, kid. There's the type cases, there's the letterpress, there's the ink, and there's the card stock; do it yourself."

After I finished my first card for Tom's Garden Service, Max flipped the card over, noted the ink had bled through the thick card stock, got a sour look on his face, and barked, "Kid! Ya put too much ink on the table! Ya ruined a great piece of stock. Don't ya know that paper is a holy thing to a printer? Oh, but you're not a printer, are you? You're just a printer's devil, put on earth to devil this old printer."

Max gently slapped me on the back and told me how to remove the excess ink I had applied to the press. I duly printed out the next ninety-nine cards in perfect fashion. That little card run didn't help me get very many gardening jobs, but it forced Max Gosseling to look at me in a different light. He learned how much I cared about paper and about him. Max rustled up more printing jobs so I would have more work to do.

I wiped the ink off my hands with solvent and a rag and walked into the front room. Max said, "Wash your hands with gritty soap and lots of hot water. We're doing a clean job next." That meant we would be working paper with our hands. It cannot be ruined with smudges or creases. Those are profane acts to printers. They defile the paper. Paper is a holy thing to a printer.

Max sat down next to me at the collating table. We stuffed envelopes with flyers. About two thousand envelopes. It was exacting, boring, and potentially dangerous work. Paper cuts were inevitable.

Max relaxed once he determined I was doing the job right. He began to speak, "Kid, did ya know that I've been married seven times?"

Tel. 225-1184
Tom's Garden Service
Lawns Mowed, Cleaned and Watered, Etc.
Honest Rates

I printed my own business card when I was about twelve. I designed, selected, proofed, and set it in three different fonts. Max selected the nineteenth-century business buzz words ("Honest Rates").

◈◈◈

This is the back side of the first card in the Tom's Garden Service run I did for myself. I applied too much ink and it bled through the stock. A typical rookie mistake.

I snorted, "No."

Max laughed too. "Yeah, I annulled two of 'em the next day. But I only had two kids. Daughters. They live in Los Angeles. They keep talkin' me into retiring. Kid, did you know I've been retired five times?"

I attempted to edge an irrelevant no into the conversation, but Max charged on with the thread: "Each time I retired, it damned near killed me. I always went back to work. I thought I was sick of printing, so I became a commercial fisherman. I lost a lot of money on that deal.

"I moved to San Jose to get away from my daughters, so they'll leave me alone. I'm almost eighty goddamned years old. If I want to work until the day I drop dead, then that's my own goddamned business, ain't it, kid?"

That must have been a rhetorical question, because Max didn't give me a chance to answer. He said, "Besides. I have a lot of fun. I go to the movies every night. There aren't very many theaters in this town. They don't change the movies often enough. That means I have to watch the same movies over and again, the ones in color anyway. I won't watch a black-and-white movie, that's the past. Color's the future, kid. Remember that."

Max told me that color was the coming thing at least a thousand times. How could I ever forget?

Max continued, "Did you know I saw *Cleopatra* 137 times?"

I knew Max went to the movies a lot, but that theatrical statistic caught me by surprise. I laughed out loud. "Why?"

"Because it's in color. Beautiful living color. It's got the best color of any movie that's in the theaters right now. Beautiful color. That's the stuff, eh, kid? Just like the flyers we're stuffing."

When Max finally took a breath, I managed to sneak in a question: "Did you know my aunt Betty is in *Cleopatra*?"

Max said, "Yeah, and I'm Willie Mays."

I said, "No, really. She was Elizabeth Taylor's body double in a bunch of movies. She was the girl who was rolled out of the carpet for Richard Burton, uh, I mean, Julius Caesar."

Max whistled and said, "Your aunt must be some hot number."

"She is. She's a stripper. The highest-paid one in Los Angeles, but she goes all over the world too. People pay a lot of money to watch her take her clothes off."

That impressed Max. He grimaced and said, "Strippers, ugh! I was married to one. They're all nuts. Is your aunt normal?"

I laughed and said, "Everyone I know says she's batshit crazy."

Max looked at me with a serious expression and said, "You stay away from strippers, kid. They just ain't worth the grief."

Max quickly shifted gears back to his movie-watching habit. He said, "What did you think of *Cleopatra*, Tommy?"

I said, "I've never seen it. Frank doesn't let us go to that kind of movie. He likes war movies, cowboy movies, he-man stuff. He won't watch a movie where men walk around bare-legged, wearing sandals or togas. He says he won't spend his hard-earned money to watch a bunch of faggots prance around a movie screen."

Max was quiet for a moment. I could tell he didn't know how to deal with Frank's views on actors, movies, and sexual standards. After a while, Max said, "Kid, would ya like to see your aunt Betty in *Cleopatra*? I'd like to see it again. We could go tonight."

I said, "Wow! That would be cool. Let me go home and take a bath first. I need to wash off the printer's ink."

"I got news for you, kid. You've already got printer's ink in your veins. You ain't never gonna be able to wash it off."

Max and I finished the envelopes. We packed them into boxes. I wrapped the boxes with glossy paper. The packages went into

Max's car. He said, "You run along home now. I'm gonna deliver this order. I'll see you back here at seven."

I quickly rode home. I did my evening chores, fed the animals and myself, then took a bath. At five minutes to seven, I was standing in front of Max's trailer.

Since this was a social call, I knocked on the door. Max stepped outside. He was wearing a beautiful light brown fedora. Max saw me staring at the hat and said, "It keeps my head warm." It also changed his appearance. I couldn't see his huge, bulbous head. He looked human, not like a Martian.

Max said, "Well, what are ya waitin' for, kid? Get in the car."

Max's car was a 1964 Ford Thunderbird. With two passengers and a full tank of gas, it weighed two and a half tons. It required a lot of power to nudge that wallowing pig down the road. Ford's 390-cubic-inch V-8 engine was up to the task; it produced 315 horsepower and almost 400 foot-pounds of torque.

Why am I waxing poetic about a bad car? To set up a story. I had ridden with Max Gosseling in his car many times over the years. The trip to see *Cleopatra* was the last. We were northbound on Monterey Highway, headed for downtown San Jose. That's where most of the movie theaters were located. When we approached Lewis Road, a car crossed the intersection directly in front of us. There was no danger. It wasn't really a close call. The other driver was just being a jerk.

Well, that pissed Max off. He loudly exclaimed, "Goddamned sons of bitches." I heard Max use that term many times. It was his favorite descriptor for a dishonorable person. Truth be told, I always suppressed my laughter when Max delivered his "sons of bitches" line. He was trying to be serious but failed. His delivery was tragically comic.

But I wasn't quite ready for what happened this time Max spoke that line: He floored the gas pedal. The transmission down-shifted, and the huge V-8 engine screamed to the red line. The four-barrel carburetor sucked air like a hurricane and sounded like a howling banshee.

Now, some people might say that 1964 Ford Thunderbirds are slow. Yeah, that's right, when you consider their performance from a dead stop. But we were traveling about 45 miles per hour when Max hit the gas. That monster car took off like a scared cat. Max cleared the rear bumper of the guy who cut us off by about an inch.

I came from a family of famous race car drivers, wannabe race car drivers, and drunks. I had seen lots of scary driving, but this was the first time I saw someone purposely attempt to ram another car. I was screaming my lungs out. I thought we were going to die.

Max let off the gas and didn't say another word. But he was gripping the steering wheel with his strong-man hands. His face bore the look of the Nordic god Thor. Max Gosseling was armed and ready to dispense vengeance.

I knew this was a good time to suppress my opinions. Anything I said would only make matters worse.

Max calmed down by the time we got to the theater. His face lit up when he saw the posters in front of the theater. He pointed and said, "Look at that wonderful color, kid. And look at the quality of the printing. Wonderful registration. It's right on. I can't believe how much better printing has gotten."

I agreed. This was a far cry from the business cards I printed on Max's hand-operated, nineteenth-century letterpresses.

But I didn't want to talk about printing right now. I had spent the day working in a printshop. I wanted to see my aunt Betty up on the screen. I changed the subject, "Thank you for bringing me to see *Cleopatra*, Max."

"No problem, kid. Let's go inside."

I rated *Cleopatra* as an okay but not great movie. That was mostly because Elizabeth Taylor was in it. I didn't like her. *Cleopatra* enabled me to see why. She reminded me of my aunt Betty. Beautiful, intelligent, vain, alcoholic—and explosive. But the lack of artistic merit didn't bother me at all. Why? Because I was only there to see Aunt Betty get rolled out of the carpet.

Once that moment passed, it was all a bore to me. Max was fidgeting in his seat. I could tell he was bored too. I remember thinking maybe viewing number 138 cured him of his *Cleopatra* habit. Max caught my eye. He whispered, "Ya wanna scram, kid?"

I nodded my head and got out of my seat. We exited the theater. Max said, "What did ya think of that, kid? Great stuff, eh?"

I said, "Yes, it was."

Max said, "And what did you think of your aunt's bit?"

I said, "Yes, that was Betty, no denying that."

Max gave me a quizzical look. I could tell he was wondering how I knew what my aunt's body looked like.

I had seen many nude photos of Betty over the years. They were better than most I saw in *Playboy*. But I couldn't tell Max any of that. I smiled, shrugged my shoulders, and walked to the car.

We didn't talk much on the way home. We were tired. It had been a long day in the printshop.

I went to Max's a few days later. He had a job for me. But I was startled by what I saw in front of the trailer: Max's Thunderbird was smashed. It had major front-end damage. I went into the trailer. Max didn't say much. He told me about the task of the day and shut up.

What's the name
of this cat?
Oh yeah!
"Lolita"
Love — Eliza (Betty)

My aunt Betty in all her stripper glory. The nipple-covering doodads she is wearing are called pasties. Betty was known as "The Queen of the Tassels," so Betty's pasties suffered a great deal of wear and tear. When she was pressed for time, sometimes Betty asked me to help repair her costumes—especially the pasties. Things went on like that until it finally occurred to Betty that what I was doing wasn't age-appropriate. She looked at me and said, "I don't really think that's something a fifteen-year-old boy should be doing." I looked up from my work, but didn't miss a beat. "Oh, Betty, don't you think it's a bit late for us to be having this discussion?" I looked down and made another attempt to secure a dangling sequin on Betty's pastie.

◇◇◇

The details of Betty's inscription to my mother is revealing. It reads: "What's the name of this cat? Oh yeah! Lo'lita. Love—Eliza (Betty)." My future mother was supposed to be named Lolita, but the county clerk in Spiro, Oklahoma, didn't know how to spell that exotic name. The clerk substituted Bernice as the first name on the official birth certificate. The family didn't care; they thought Lolita was too much of a mouthful anyway. They called my future mother Lita. When she was in her sixties, Lita officially changed the hated Bernice to Loeta. Still and all, my mother lived as a sexual Lolita for most of her life. Circa 1965.

Betty with her husband and sap of a lifetime, Kenneth Kirkley. Betty hated men, was a stone-cold genius, and turned mean as a snake when she was drunk, which was pretty much always. The police in Fairbanks, Alaska, referenced my aunt on their radios on a first-name basis, such as, "Betty is at it, again at the XYZ bar" or "Betty is raising hell down at the steak house." Betty inevitably became abusive with everybody she was with for more than about fifteen minutes—excepting Lita.

I once saw Lita get into a full-on fight with five young cowboys in a Texas beer joint. The cowboys were trying; Lita won. Few sane people fucked with Lita more than once. My aunt Betty wasn't quite as crazy as she wanted people to believe.

CLOSE COVER BEFORE STRIKING · FOR SAFETY
2 BLKS. N. OF RICKEYS
4120 EL CAMINO, PALO ALTO
PH. 327-9901
FROM 9 P.M.
TUES. thru SUN.
EXOTIC DANCERS
featuring
CAMEO CLUB
FLOOR SHOW NITELY

⬦⬦⬦

Legal strip clubs were a new thing in early 1960s California. San Francisco had a few and there was one down south, in Palo Alto: the Cameo Club. That is where Betty hit the stripper big leagues. She was the Cameo Club headliner for a couple of years, then moved on to higher-paying San Francisco venues. The Cameo Club put Betty on the cover of their giveaway matchbooks in about 1963. They used that matchbook for as long as they were in business.

Later, he quietly said, "The goddamned sons of bitches are always cutting me off."

That was it. The full explanation of Max's wreck. I shivered and thought: Oh, boy, Tommy. There ain't no way on god's green earth you're getting in a car with him again.

Truth be told, I never got another chance to ride in a car with Max Gosseling. Here's how that worked out. Max was quite busy during that period. People liked the quality of his printed goods. He was great at rush orders, the king of the twenty-four-hour-print-job turnaround. This created a lot of work for me. So it was that I was able to see three wrecked 1964 Ford Thunderbirds parked in front of Max's trailer in as many weeks! There were no cars parked in front of Max's trailer after the fourth week. The Department of Motor Vehicles had revoked his driver's license.

You might think that a lack of wheels would slow an eighty-year-old man. It didn't. Max hired cabs. He picked up paper and ink in cabs. He hauled lead type and delivered orders in cabs. He went to the movies every night in cabs. Max Gosseling was on a first-name basis with every taxi driver in town.

None of those occurrences changed anything for me. Max and I kept a comfortable rhythm. It seemed to be timeless. I accomplished all sorts of jobs for him. He tuned my fingers and my brain. He paid me well. I ate food when I was hungry, and I bought better toys all the time. I renewed the subscription to *Playboy* that one of my aunts gave me when I was fourteen. But there was an unexpected side effect from all that; I forged a friendship of sorts with Max Gosseling. He and I were quite close, though neither of us ever admitted it.

18

THE END OF THE GRAND TIMES

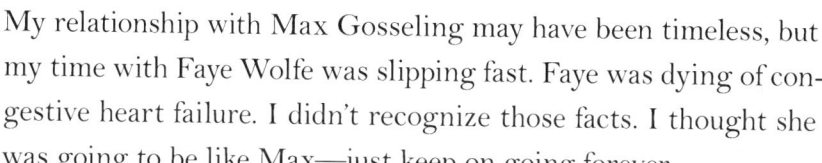

My relationship with Max Gosseling may have been timeless, but my time with Faye Wolfe was slipping fast. Faye was dying of congestive heart failure. I didn't recognize those facts. I thought she was going to be like Max—just keep on going forever.

I went to Faye's house every day. I filled the wood box and stoked the fire. I carried out the trash and pulled weeds in the garden. More of our visits were occurring in Faye's bedroom. She was too sick to rise. But her face always brightened when she saw me. She always got the same elf-like twinkle in her eye I saw on our first day.

When Faye was feeling better, we sat on the iron bench, just like old times. Our visits there were briefer now. Faye couldn't bear to sit for very long.

We finally got to what turned out to be our last visit in that place. To me, it seemed just like countless others, which stretched back over the years. But Faye's cheerful words were just a set-up; she quickly got to the meat of the conversation: "Tommy. Take the strawberry pot. Take the Santa Maria ship model and the little jug with the gold dust. Take them home. Now!"

I clenched my eyes shut, furiously shook my head from side to side and said, "No. No. NO! I won't. They're yours. You need them!"

Faye quietly said, "Listen to me, Tommy. I'd love to leave you all this—the house, the land, the little stove—all of it. But I owe money to the county for all those years I spent on welfare. I owe money to the daughter of my last lover. Those people are going to swoop down on this place like vultures when I die. They would fight you tooth and nail over the tiniest scrap. I don't want you to endure that. You already have enough hardship in your life."

I felt the weight of the world on my shoulders at that moment. I finally got it: Faye was about to die. She was my only real friend. I didn't want to talk about pots and houses and ships and stuff like that.

I looked down at my lap. I didn't know what to say. I tried not to show my tears but failed. I'm no good at hiding them.

Faye broke the silence. "Please take the strawberry pot home today—at least."

I nodded my head and said, "Yes. I would like to have that. It would help me to remember you. But the ship model and jug are too old and precious. They belong in a museum."

Faye snorted and said, "They will end up in a junk store, sold for spite. I'm worn out from all this talk about death. It feels like I'm walking on my own grave. It's bad luck. Go home. Take the pot with you. Come back tomorrow. I will feel better. We'll have a grand time then."

I helped Faye get into bed. I fed the stove and closed the door. I rode my bike home. I returned to Faye's house with a wheelbarrow and bundle of burlap sacks. I padded the wheelbarrow bottom with some of the sacks and wrapped the strawberry pot with others. I tied the sacks with jute twine. I thought, now comes the hard part. I've got to lift this heavy sucker. I was glad that Faye waited so long to give me the strawberry pot. It required every bit of my strength to lift it into the wheelbarrow.

I wheeled the strawberry pot home. It was a short but nerve-wracking trip. I was worried the strawberry pot would tip and roll out of the wheelbarrow. That almost happened a couple of times. Luck and well-practiced wheelbarrow skills carried me through. I unloaded the strawberry pot on our patio. It looked forlorn and out of place in that tacky suburban space. I remember thinking, old pot, I wish you and I could spend eternity on Faye Wolfe's front porch, but that just ain't a gonna happen. It's you and me now.

I tried to tell folks about my new treasure, but no one wanted to hear it. One of my teachers laughed in my face. She said I was exaggerating about the pot's importance. Other kids claimed their dad, mom, or uncle had a better strawberry pot. Frank and Lita weren't around, so I couldn't tell them anything. I thought, that's okay. Faye knows how special it is. I'll talk to her about it.

I went to Faye's house after school the next day. She didn't answer my knock on the side door. I stood back and looked at the chimney; no smoke was emerging. I walked around to the front door and clanged the bell several times. No answer. I rang again. The echoes of the last beat lost themselves in the eucalyptus trees. I have never heard a lonelier sound. I knew something was wrong. Where was Faye? I was worried.

I went home and tried to keep my mind off Faye. It was tough. My animals, garden, books, and music just couldn't hold my attention. At about eight in the evening, the telephone rang. I ran across the room to answer it. It was Faye. She said, "Tommy, I'm in the county hospital."

The Wolfe strawberry pot on my patio, April 2019. This pot was created by people who made useful clay objects. Their pieces were generally thick-walled and roughly finished, not thin, light, and beautiful like the many commonly found in art galleries and pottery outlets. Carl Wolfe's workers used high-quality clay, then fired the pieces at much higher temperatures than are used on terra-cotta. The Carl Wolfe strawberry pot is much harder than most terra-cotta objects. It rings like a bell when you thump it with your finger. This pot was made to be used; it holds a lot of soil and has a very large top opening. That detail was important to old-time gardeners. Why? A large top opening holds more water. Old-time gardeners didn't have water hoses. They sequentially filled their pots with a can, then moved on to other tasks.

◇◇◇

Handprints and fingerprints on the Wolfe strawberry pot. I believe these were made when the potter moved the pot from the workroom to the drying shed. The potter had small hands.

"I'm coming over right now. I'll ride my bike. It's only six miles. I know the way. I was born there."

Faye began to wail—a thin, keening lament. She said, "Oh, my god, no, Tommy. I look terrible. You wouldn't recognize me. I don't want you to see me like this."

I tried to say something, but Faye cut me off. "I have to go now. Someone else needs the phone. I just wanted to tell you that you are my one and only lovey. You have been my heart and soul for many years. Thank you." Faye was crying as she hung up the telephone.

I lost my mind. I dropped to the floor and began wailing. My dog didn't know what was going on. He began to howl and dig madly on the patio door. He wanted to be with me. When I collected myself, I went outside and snuggled the poor dog. He was bereft. I stared at the strawberry pot on the other side of the patio. That sight brought me little comfort; it just reminded me more of Faye.

After a time, I went back inside. My cat was waiting. He was concerned too. I picked him up and went to the bedroom and collapsed on the bed. I couldn't stop thinking about Faye. I didn't want to think about life without Faye. My cat curled up next to me. His purring rumble lulled me to sleep.

That welcome respite lasted all night. I woke the next morning. The cat was still there. I petted him for a few seconds, then remembered Faye. I jumped out of bed and ran to the telephone. I called the county hospital. The operator transferred me to Faye's ward. The nurse who answered the phone was brusque and rude. I could tell she was sick of receiving phone calls from the families of indigent patients.

I asked, "How is Mrs. Wolfe doing?"

The nurse barked, "She died," and slammed down the phone. That was it. Boom. Over. Faye was dead.

I was stunned. I stood like a statue, the telephone handset hanging from my left hand. I didn't cry, wail, or think. I just stood there. The telephone's insistent off-hook signal snapped me out of my daze. I slowly replaced the handset on the cradle. It was a crushing blow. Faye was everything to me. I had just two real friends during that period of my life. The other was a seventeen-year-old boy who died a few months before Faye.

No one was at home to console me. I was alone. I eventually called my grandmother, but it was laundry day. She didn't have time to listen to my problems. My grandmother abruptly said, "Hush up now. You ought to be ashamed of yourself, the way you're carrying on. You're nearly a grown man now. Men don't cry. My clothes are getting wrinkled in the washer." She hung up the phone without saying goodbye.

I saw Frank and Lita a few days later. They were having a big fight. Frank had spent his check at the bar, again. He came home smelling like cheap perfume, again. When I tried to interject my news about Faye, they turned on me and told me how selfish I was, that I was always thinking about myself. Frank ended those thoughts by saying, "Get in your room. Don't come out till I tell you to."

Frank didn't tell me to come out until the next morning. The sad expression on my face provided the excuse he needed to go off on me. He said, "I'm embarrassed to see you a carryin' on about a worn-out ol' whore this way. She ain't worth the grief. Anyway, men don't act like that. Men don't cry."

I tried to explain the depth of my loss, but Frank cut me off by saying, "If you don't get a happy look on your ugly fuckin' face

◇◇◇

Lita worked every minute of overtime Lockheed would give her, but it was never enough to replenish Frank's bottomless party fund. She did everything she could to make more money.

Lita hosted gift parties, crocheted poodle-dog covers on empty whiskey bottles from the Rock Castle bar, and sold bras. The latter activity fit right in with the Lita's exaggerated sexuality. It also gave her more opportunities to cock-tease me. Lita walked into my room, pirouetted and announced, "Tommy, this is a new bra style. Do you think the straps are properly adjusted?" When it got to the point where Lita wanted me to adjust her bra straps, I walked out of the house.

right quick like, I'm a gonna give ya somethin' to really be sad about." Frank grinned as he spoke those words. He clenched and unclenched his fists several times, getting them loosened up, so he could grab and pummel me better.

I forced a smile on my face and said, "You're right. I need to get over it." I turned and walked away. I was happy to have escaped being pummeled by Frank, but I was still sad.

Lita was a little more sympathetic, until I asked her to take me to Faye's funeral. Don't get me wrong, Lita adored Faye, but didn't want to take time off from work to get me to the funeral. Lita was working a lot of overtime. She had to replenish Frank's bottomless party fund.

Lita told her friends and relatives all about her plans to take me to Faye's funeral. She did that every time she accomplished something out of the ordinary for me. But Lita's subsequent actions revealed more truth than her self-congratulatory words. She left work at the last minute. She was stuck in heavy traffic all the way home. Lita was a raging maniac by the time she drove into our driveway.

She honked the car horn, over and again. That action was gratuitous. She did not need to summon me from inside the house. I had been standing in front of the house for half an hour. I was in tears. I knew that Faye's funeral had already begun. But none of that mattered to Lita. When she finally saw that I was already in the front yard, she began a long stream of incomprehensible invective. She paused her spiel long enough to scream, "Get your ass in the fuckin' car! We're late!"

I ran to the car and opened the door. Lita slammed the car into reverse and hit the gas before I was inside. The door slammed against me. I almost fell out of the car. I was stunned.

That gave Lita the excuse she needed to go off on me. "Quit fuckin' around over there! Watch out what you're doin' to my car! Don't tear the fuckin' seat! Why do you have to be so fuckin' clumsy? Why do I always have to take fuckin' time off from work for you?"

I didn't bother to answer. I knew they were rhetorical questions, carefully hurled weapons. But for once, the sting in Lita's words didn't find its mark. I was grieving for Faye. At that moment, I didn't give a shit what Lita thought about anything. I slumped down in the seat. I tried to make myself invisible, make Lita forget I was there.

Lita quickly proved that my feelings were irrelevant. She moved on to another point: "There's a bottle in the top of my purse. Take out one of the pills and give it to me."

That request surprised me. Lita's purse was a holy thing. God help any man, woman, or child who delved into Lita's purse without asking. They might not live to tell about what they found inside. For that reason, I proceeded carefully, like I was walking on eggshells. I carefully lifted a bottle of prescription tranquilizers. I removed one pill. I handed it to Lita, and she popped it into her mouth.

"I wish I had some fuckin' water to wash this bastard down with, it's bitter."

I didn't say shit. I was still trying to make myself invisible.

Lita drove like a crazy woman. We sped through the cemetery gates at about 40 miles per hour. The cemetery peacocks scattered. Oak Hill is a big place. Lita had no idea where Faye's gravesite was located. Lita frantically raced up and down the narrow roads. She kept a running commentary while she raced around, "I can't believe I'm givin' you the grand tour of this fuckin' place. I can't believe I had to take off work for your fuckin' lazy ass, again!"

Lita finally noted a small knot of people on the opposite side of the cemetery. She reversed the car and backed onto a grave. She spun the tires as she drove forward. Dirt, gravel, and chunks of flying turf marked our progress. Lita sped across the cemetery and locked the brakes as we arrived at the gravesite. The car slid about six feet on the gravel and wet grass. The group turned and stared at our spectacular arrival. Lita and I arrived alongside Faye's grave just as an unknown preacher said, "Amen." We had missed the entire service.

A second glance revealed a sad fact; we didn't miss much. A handful of mourners was standing around Faye's coffin. Eva the housekeeper was there with her current lover and a few of her children. Eli wasn't part of the main group. He stood off to one side, all by himself. His face was a veil of tears. Eli was semi-comatose from the effects of strong drink, but he was silent. I was thankful for that small grace. I had seen lots of drunks get rowdy at funerals.

The daughter of Faye's last lover was there. She glowered at me when I approached. She didn't say hello or offer me a handshake. That woman preferred a direct approach, the full salvo. "Faye wanted me to give you a bunch of stuff from her house, but I'm not. It's valuable. That crazy old whore cost me a lot of money." The woman raised her chin into the air, shot me a smug look, spun on her heels, and walked away.

The preacher watched that sorry little speech but didn't say a word. I suppose he was used to hearing such things. He walked over to me, stuck out his hand, and said, "You must be Tommy. Faye thought the world of you."

I took his hand and said, "Thank you."

The preacher said, "I know that Faye specifically asked for a closed casket, but would you like to see her, anyway, one last time?" He walked to the coffin and placed his hand on the edge of the lid. He was getting ready to raise it when I spun around, faced the departing mourners, and cried, "Why is everybody around here trying to do what Faye didn't want?" The mourners paused and stared at me like I was a freak show geek, but I didn't care. I loved Faye Wolfe more than anything else on earth.

The casket stayed closed.

Lita chose that moment to begin acting like a mother. Folks who knew her well might say the tranquilizer had finally kicked in. I saw her behavior for what it was—an act. Lita only behaved like a mother when she had an audience. She wrapped her arms around me and said, "It's okay, Tommy. You know you did the right thing."

Faye's funeral program is a real doozy; it gets two facts wrong; Faye was born in 1881, not 1891. I know this is true, because Faye gave me an 1881 Liberty quarter. She said; "Tommy, you will always remember when I died. Please take this coin so you will remember when I was born."

Then, there's the other funeral program error; Faye was born in Deadwood, South Dakota, not Kansas. Carl Wolfe was born in Kansas. What is the reason for the funeral program errors? The daughter of Faye's last lover hated Faye. The lover's daughter thought Faye was "a conniving old leech who should have been dead ten years ago." I only met the lover's daughter a handful of times over the years. She was brusque with Faye and rudely dismissive of me. The lover's daughter was concerned that Faye would change her will to give me the gatekeeper's cottage. She didn't have anything to worry about; I didn't care about money and Faye didn't want to saddle me with the burdens that went with the cottage and its numerous encumbrances.

Any way you cut it, the lover's daughter didn't take the time to discover the true facts about Faye. History is written by the victors.

Max Gosseling walked up to me. He must have been standing off to one side, because I hadn't seen him before. Max shook my hand and said, "I'm awful sorry about Faye, kid. She really was something."

"Thank you, Max."

Max beamed and said, "You're right. You do need to thank me for coming here. I don't like funerals. I didn't even go to my own mother's funeral."

Lita interrupted our interlude. She reverted to her default setting—the best employee that Lockheed Missiles and Space ever had. She chirped, "Oh, Mr. Gosseling, would you mind if Tommy shared your taxi to get back home? It's out of my way and I've got to get back to work. The company doesn't like it when I'm gone too long."

Max said, "Sure."

Lita kissed me on the cheek and left the gravesite. Max stared at Lita's legs as she sashayed toward the car. He gave a low whistle, shook his head, and said, "Wow! What a number."

Everybody loved Lita.

Max gently slapped me on the back and said, "Come on, kid, I've got a big order to get out and a press that needs cleaning. I'm going to use yellow ink."

IN MEMORY OF
MRS. FAYE WOLFE

BORN
April 13, 1891
Kansas

DEPARTED THIS LIFE
April 24, 1966
San Jose, California

SERVICES HELD
Wednesday, April 27, 1966 at 11:00 A. M.
OAK HILL MEMORIAL PARK

CLERGYMAN OFFICIATING
The Reverend Gottfried Stone

INTERMENT
OAK HILL MEMORIAL PARK

Faye's tombstone has two names, two dates, and one error.

◇◇◇

Faye's funeral program gets two facts wrong: Faye was born in 1881, not 1891, in South Dakota, not Kansas.

19

LIFE AFTER FAYE

I had a lot of free time on my hands after Faye died. I looked for things to do after school. When I was a high school sophomore, I became the official scorekeeper for our school basketball team. That was a difficult, important, stressful job. Referees checked the official league scorebook several times during the game. Our coach studied the book like a bible, whether it was a league game or not. I had to be right all the time, every time.

My scorekeeper's job didn't end after the games were over. I phoned the scores to the night sports reporter at the *San Jose Mercury-News.* He was a harried junior staffer who took about thirty calls from other league basketball scorekeepers in an hour's time on game nights.

The first time I phoned the scores, the sportswriter set the rules: "Listen up; it's only a couple of hours until we put the morning edition to bed. I don't have time to write a bunch of piddly assed articles about high school ball scores. I like it when the scorekeepers write the articles, though most don't. You sound like a smart kid, so I'm gonna expect more from you. I'll correct your blurbs [articles] for grammar and diction, but I expect you to dictate good copy, every time. Got it? If you can't do that, I'll find another kid to phone the scores from your school."

I suppose some scorekeepers were intimidated by the reporter's rant. Not me. The reporter didn't know I had been working for a manic, perfectionist printer for almost five years. Max Gosseling said, "Kid! Follow your copy out the window!" Let me translate that from printer-speak: Write appropriate copy, then set type that exactly matches the copy. Reporting for the *Mercury-News* was easy; I didn't have to set type for my articles or clean the presses afterward.

Max didn't always have a lot of work for me to do, but I didn't stop needing money. When I was fifteen, I began to look for additional after-school jobs. I found one at the egg ranch, which was located on the other side of the mountain Faye once owned.

I fed chickens, collected eggs, and shoveled chicken shit—mountains of chicken shit. As time went on, I began to suspect the ranch owners only kept me around because they needed someone to shovel shit. When I got tired of that activity, I talked the owners into letting me sell their eggs at the San Jose Flea Market. I worked for hours on a crude, hand-lettered sign. Alas, it was all for naught; we sold few eggs that day.

The next day, it was back to shoveling chicken shit for me. Truth be told, I didn't mind. The egg ranch owners stood next to me, shoveling along.

I was one of a handful of kids who rode a bike to our large high school. It was considered uncool at that time to ride a bicycle. Some kids walked for miles to avoid the stigma of being "a dumb ol' bike rider." I didn't have a choice; I had to ride a bike to and from school. Why? Because I played four brass instruments in five different groups. At one point, I was also tenor drummer in

Hill 53,
Ayer 49

MILPITAS — Ayer had Hill down all the way until ate in the fourth period when theFalcons employed a full-court press and long field goals by Chris Mounton to provide a 53-49 Mount Hamilton League basketball victory for Hill and remain in contention for the league title.

Henry Williams and Manny Martinez tied Hill's Cornell Burris for high point honors with 15 tallies while Moulton has 12 and Tom Borup 10 for Hill.

One of my first articles in a major publication. Circa 1966.

◇◇◇

One of the egg ranch owners and his son are on the left side of this photograph with me and a flat of unsold eggs at the San Jose Flea Market. Summer 1966.

another musical group. Any way you cut it, I was hauling a lot of heavy brass over the long miles between home and school.

Lita bought me a Schwinn that had heavy-duty racks on the front and back. I made a funny sight going down the road, with two or three instrument cases wedged onto and around my bike and one banging against my knees. The selection of instruments I hauled varied according to the musical season, but one was never absent: a French horn.

The horn was the main love that replaced Faye in my life. Before her death, I spent one to three hours with Faye, every day. After she died, I practiced the horn for one to two hours. I might also practice a euphonium, trumpet, or British bugle for an hour, but the horn was what really got my love. I didn't own any of the horns I played in high school. They were loaners I got through my high school band teacher, Michael Kambeitz.

At first, Mike loaned me the Reynolds horn the air force supplied him to play in one of their bands. It was heavy, had an awful tone, and was difficult to control above high C. Mike persuaded a local music store to loan me what was reputed to be the first Yamaha French horn that was imported into America. It was like driving a new Mercedes-Benz after a twenty-five-year old Toyota. I had the Yamaha for a year, and then the music store wanted it back. I was bummed.

Would I have to play the wretched air force horn again? Mike didn't allow that to happen; he loaned me the horn of a lifetime. I won't tell you the brand, but I will tell you what the horn was made of: *goldmessing*. That term translates from German as "gold brass." The brass in my loaner horn was alloyed with about 10 to 20 percent gold, by weight. The little golden horn played like a dream and sang like an angel—a better instrument than I was a player. It was a curious thing to be a child who sometimes went hungry while playing a horn that contained several pounds of pure gold. The pint-sized philosopher in me couldn't fail to miss the irony of the moment.

I was drum major of the Prince Charles Pipe Band for several years during and after high school. That position was not as prestigious as it might seem. You see, drum majors don't really do anything in pipe bands except stand out front, wave long objects, and try to look more decorative than ridiculous. No joke. The Pipe Major runs the show. I could barely whistle the tunes. It gets worse from there. Drum majors cannot earn any points for the band during competitions, but they can do things that subtract from the band's overall score. That flawed dynamic keeps the relationship between a drum major and the band on an arm's-length basis.

I worked with Max Gosseling for about a year after Faye's death, well into my high school days. I stopped only when Frank decided to make another spur-of-the-moment move. Our new home was too far from Max's print shop for me to work for him. Mass transit was nonexistent in our area. Then Frank took us back to Texas where I showed off my skills as a printer's devil and finally graduated from high school.

In our hasty move from the Senter Road home, I left behind beloved friends in my garden. I had created fruit trees, among my many creations. One sequentially bore three peach varieties through spring and summer. It took several years of my inexperienced and indifferent care to create the harvest Lita rescued before we moved.

She hurriedly picked the half-green fruit, knowing she was about to leave her home of longest duration. Frank was pissed because Lita slowed him for fifteen minutes while she picked the fruit.

On my own in California
during my high school
senior year, living in my
1953 Buick Special.

◇◇◇

The peach tree I created, in
the background. Lita looks
grim-faced because Frank
sold the house and moved us
to an awful rental apartment.

He said, "Leave the fuckin' fruit on the tree, it ain't important. I'll buy ya'll a can of Del Monte's on the way to our new rental."

Lita discovered it was impossible to fit most of her possessions into the small trailers Frank rented for our move. When Lita complained, Frank preached the sermon he had been using on me for almost fifteen years: "You're in love with them possessions. That's a sin. You're gonna burn in hell for bein' in love with things."

Frank and Lita raged at each other, all the way. When they failed to find common cause in their argument, they turned on me. Happy first peach harvest, Tommy.

Soon thereafter, Frank decided to sell almost everything he owned and move back to Texas. I went to Texas for a couple of weeks, but quickly went back to California. I wanted to finish my final year of high school in San Jose. Frank was happy to see me gone. He had been doing his best to intimidate me out of his home since I was fourteen.

Lita was doing her typical "Stand by Your Man" routine, so she was no help. I was on my own in California, which makes me remember my 1953 Buick Special. It was the first car I ever lived in. I credit Frank McMillan for that eventuality. I ended up back in Texas to finish high school, however.

Unbeknownst to me, I had received a letter from Max in response to the Temple, Texas, high school graduation notice I sent to him. When it arrived, Lita was too busy with her own problems to give the letter to me. She stuffed it into her photo archives and went on with her miserable life.

The letter is dated May 31, 1969, but I didn't read Max's letter until fifty years later, when I was sixty-eight years old. Max used stock photo images on his high-quality letterhead, but had done the printing years before, when I worked for him. I was stunned by the quality of the typing in the letter. There is just one error and the letters are bold and clear.

Max had great typewriters—IBMs and Adlers. He could type sixty words per minute of perfect, finished copy. I frequently proofread his stuff, but rarely found an error. Max said, "Kid! Only an idiot publishes anything without running it by an editor first!"

In his letter he typed: "Thank you for the beautiful engraved Graduation announcement, I will treasure it and your letter always more than mere money, for you are truly one of the very few really worth while persons I have known."

That paragraph contains one of the three best compliments I ever received—albeit fifty years after it was written. Thanks, Lita. By the way, I helped print "the beautiful engraved Graduation announcement" at the American Printing Company in Temple, Texas. They thought I was the best printer's devil they had seen in a long time. Thank you, Max, for training me well.

I was surprised to find that Max included four photo transparencies with his 1969 letter. One is an inside view of Max's third and last house-trailer–mounted darkroom. I worked in two of them and helped to build one.

Air vents were mounted on the right side of the door. Those vents indicate Max finally got sick of breathing chemical-laden air when he worked in the darkroom. Fumes didn't seem to bother Max when I worked for him. The trailer is a Lo-Liner. That brand is especially small, light, and low. They were designed to be towed behind small cars and trucks. Max Gosseling was an expert at doing fine work in incredibly small spaces. The real kicker was that Max lived in his various trailers, alongside his beloved graphics equipment.

Max was about eighty-two when he built the mobile darkroom.

May 31st, 1969

Dear Tommy:-

You gave me the most happy surprise
I have had for years to hear from you
again.

Thanks for the beautiful engraved
Graduation announcement, I will treasure
it and your letter always more than mere
money, for you are truly one of the very
few really worth while persons I have
known.

If you expect to make a career of printing
you should save your earnings or marry a
beautiful girl with lots of talent and
capital and start your own printing plant,
as there is seldom much percentage in being
a slave.

Sold the printing business about 2 months ago.
Cleaned and remodeled the large trailer and am
trying to sell it. Now have the travel trailer
shown in the enclosed transparency which I have
converted into a very complete color laboratory,
made specially designed baffles with which it
can within minutes be converted into a black as
coal darkroom while the sun is shining. Used to
think that developing color film was terribly
complicated, the anticipation of doing this was
really the only hard part, with the proper equipment
it is like shooting fish in a rain barrel.

Wishing you and your mother the very best that life
has to offer. I am mighty proud to have known you.

Max Schaesberg

◇◇◇

Max's letter to me upon my graduation from high school.

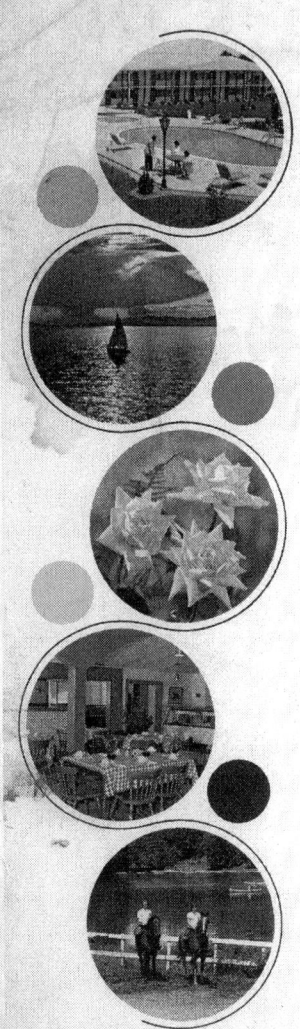

Max Gosseling
Natural Color Advertising
:·: TEL. 408-225-2732
SAN JOSE, CALIFORNIA 95111

◇◇◇

Max Gosseling's last letterhead.

He didn't have a driver's license the last few times I saw him. I don't know how he planned to tow the trailer.

I visited Max a few years after he moved from the Monterey Road trailer park. Max handed me the letterhead in the photograph. He had carefully blocked the 4210 Monterey Road address with color-matched correcting paint. The man was an artist, right to the end. He was a businessman too; Max claimed he was still "drumming up business." At that time, he was about eighty-nine years old.

Lita was descended from what is sometimes called the Indian Peach Culture. White men brought peaches to the New World in the mid-sixteenth century. It didn't take my Cherokee/Choctaw ancestors long to integrate peaches into their diet. The fruit was eaten fresh in summer and preserved for winter eating. Peaches added starch, vitamin C, sugar, and flavor to menus that sometimes lacked those essential components.

I was conceived under an apricot tree. My mother worked in the orchards and fruit packing sheds while I formed inside her belly. I was just a few days old when someone took a photo of me in an orchard. When I was a few weeks old, Lita took me with her while she worked among the trees. I could identify any type of stone fruit tree when I was three, leaves on, leaves off, I knew them all. I have spent my life searching for fruit blossoms.

If we had nothing else (and we didn't), Lita and I shared a love of the garden's bounty. In San Jose, we measured our year by the life cycle of fruit trees. Blossom time was the happiest for us.

Lita in a Vidivic cherry orchard,
Sunnyvale, California. Circa 1973.

✧✧✧

I found these fruit blossoms on Senter Road
in San Jose in the spring of 1968.

ABOUT THE AUTHOR

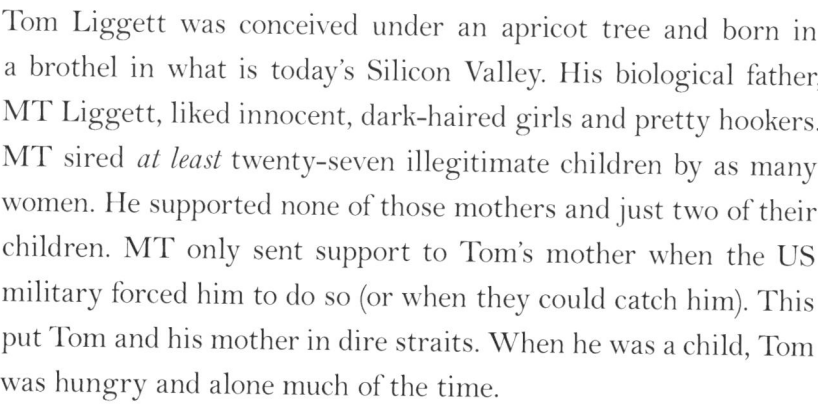

Tom Liggett was conceived under an apricot tree and born in a brothel in what is today's Silicon Valley. His biological father, MT Liggett, liked innocent, dark-haired girls and pretty hookers. MT sired *at least* twenty-seven illegitimate children by as many women. He supported none of those mothers and just two of their children. MT only sent support to Tom's mother when the US military forced him to do so (or when they could catch him). This put Tom and his mother in dire straits. When he was a child, Tom was hungry and alone much of the time.

Tom was taken into the orchard in a banana box when he was just two weeks old. His mother needed the work and refused to "waste" money on babysitters. When he was just a little older, Tom toddled around the orchards and fruit processing sheds. When Tom was three, he could identify the various stone fruit types.

Age eleven was a pivotal time in young Tom's life. He was an old hand at reading and interpreting college-level horticultural texts. That was when he began to accomplish rudimentary plant research projects in his suburban ghetto backyard. Tom also began to work. He needed money for food, toys, books, and music. Tom knew that hard work was the only avenue that led to eating regularly.

He worked as a gardener, house cleaner, apartment painter, printer's devil, fry cook, and egg ranch laborer before he got out of high school. Not long after that, he became a dishwasher, busboy, fry cook, head cook, brothel cook, and sous chef. Tom's early jobs centered around kitchens. Why? Because when he worked in kitchens, he ate. When he didn't work in kitchens, he didn't always eat.

When Tom was in school, he played in musical groups so he could have a social life. He played five brass instruments. Tom played the French horn in a symphony orchestra. He was a member of two bagpipe bands (the drum major of one).

Tom won numerous awards for speech and dramatic arts during his last few weeks of high school. He won an honorable mention for acting in the 1969 Texas state championship. That was an unusual award for an actor from a play that only came in second. It was a *really* big deal for Tom; a few weeks before that competition, he was two thousand miles away, living in a car.

Later on, Tom worked as a boilermaker, electrician, car salesman, tree cutter, nurseryman, maintenance man, weed cutter, and farmer.

He graduated from the Aerospace School of Medicine and completed bench-level special chemistry research projects for the

Surgeon General of the Air Force. He was briefly in the last class of the Army Reserve Officers' Training Corps at Stanford University.

In the midst of his occupational chaos, Tom managed to become Apple Computer employee number 114. Tom oversaw a staff of hundreds and had the only unlimited charge account in the company ("You never knew when I might have to get the manager of the local hardware store out of bed so I could buy some emergency supplies."). Tom had one of just twenty private offices at Apple and, as Tom said, "That was good, because my office contained two full-sized couches. I didn't want to stop working long enough to go home for sleep."

He has been a minor-league writer since he was sixteen. From 1966 through 1968, he had a weekly column on high school basketball scores in the *San Jose Mercury-News* ("four column inches"). Tom has written countless articles on gardening for small publications and collaborated on two books. He has published two books previous to this one: *The Pregnant Majorette* and *How to Prune, Train and Tie Rose Plants.*

Tom founded the San Jose Heritage Rose Garden, the second largest public rose garden in the world. He was chief rosarian for another major public rose garden. He has built and maintained countless private rose gardens. Tom has worked for many different nurseries. He has owned three successful nurseries and has three private gardens of his own. As Tom said, "I liked growing plants and gardens for other people. But I grew weary of creating beauty for other people while my own gardens looked like ugly truck yards."

He now grows plants only for his friends, family, and himself. He grows much of his own food. He also remembers what it was like to be hungry, so he grows tons of top-quality produce to feed the hungry. Tom operates the last full-spectrum working farm in downtown San Jose. He doesn't sell anything, except during a couple of annual charity plant sales.

Tom is currently accomplishing a research project with roses, lettuce, melons, Asian vegetables, and minor cut crops (long-stemmed flowers other than roses). He is doing great things with florists' carnations. He continues to propagate and grow eight-foot-tall tree roses ("cascades"). Tom said, "I'm the only person in the Western Hemisphere who grows large quantities of cascades in the ancient European way."

Tom observed wistfully, "I am the last classically trained, full-spectrum American rosarian. How can I know that? Because the mechanism to create more like me has been dismantled. The various rose industries I once supported are gone. The great rosarians are dead. The rose growing hobby is a shadow of its former self. This makes me sad. There used to be ten rosarians like me in every generation. I am the final link in a teacher/student chain that stretches back several hundred years."

Tom lives with his wife, dog, cats, and gardens in Silicon Valley, San Jose, California.

Made in the USA
Columbia, SC
25 January 2020